SCALING down

SCALING down

LIVING LARGE in a smaller space

Judi Culbertson and Marj Decker
illustrations by George Booth

RODALE

Printed in the United States of America
Rodale Inc. makes every effort to use acid-free ♾, recycled paper ♻.

Book design by Anthony Serge
Illustrations by George Booth
Cover photo by Craig Aurness/CORBIS

Thanks to Neil D. Armstrong, copyright coordinator, University of Minnesota Extension Service, for permission to quote from "Who Gets Grandma's Yellow Pie Plate?" (page 105). For additional information, visit www.yellowpieplate.umn.edu.

Library of Congress Cataloging-in-Publication Data

Culbertson, Judi.
    Scaling down : living large in a smaller space / Judi Culbertson and Marj Decker ; illustrations by George Booth.
        p.   cm.
    Includes bibliographical references and index.
    ISBN-13 978–1–59486–093–5 paperback
    ISBN-10 1–59486–093–9 paperback
    1. House cleaning.   2. Home economics.   I. Decker, Marj.   II. Title.
TX324.C74   2005
640—dc22   2004027372

Distributed to the trade by Holtzbrinck Publishers

  4   6   8   10   9   7   5   3   paperback

We inspire and enable people to improve their lives and the world around them
For more of our products visit **rodalestore.com** or call 800-848-4735

To our clients past, present, and future:
Without you, our work would have been much less fun!

----

contents

- →

"Today is the day I start the new me!"

INTRODUCTION

Americans are in the middle of a weight crisis—no, we're not talking about too many french fries, we're talking about *stuff.* Almost everyone has more things than they can easily keep track of or find room for. But it doesn't become a crisis until you decide to move to a condo or an apartment in the city, or retire and want to set up a part-time business office or art studio in your current home. Or you suddenly need to sort through the belongings of an older family "saver" who is moving to assisted living. Or you're simply tired of the sprawl and want to live more lightly or compactly in environmentally sound ways.

Over the years, as professional organizers, we have worked with people in similar situations doing everything from rearranging furniture to putting photographs in albums, from packing up their belongings for a move to moving pack rats emotionally from "overwhelmed" to "sane." Our clients have ranged from people who felt so motivated (or embarrassed) that they stayed up till 3:00 A.M. the night before we came tossing things out, to people initially unwilling to discard a single bent hanger.

But we have found that just getting rid of possessions and scaling down physically is not enough. In order to be successful, you need to have a direction, a positive goal—whether it is a beautiful, more compact space, a functional workshop, a sense of freedom and control, or the joy of financially exchanging "stuff" for new experiences and pleasures. To do this, we have used a Mission Statement with our clientele, and we will take you through the process as well. This, as well as the techniques we suggest, can help you overcome the inevitable roadblocks. Because people tend to remember personal stories rather than just theory, we have included many examples.

There are practical reasons to go through the scaling-down process. But we are also promising you a simply beautiful home, filled only with what you love and use, a place that uses every inch of space the way you want. We are offering you control over your environment and freedom from chaos—as well as a chance to complete a task for someone else, which you may not be looking forward to, in a way that is, ultimately, satisfying.

By the time you finish this book, your home, old or new, and the way you look at "stuff" will be forever changed. So let's get started!

part 1

THE CHALLENGE
OF SCALING DOWN

"I understand the house is a mess inside."

HOW DID WE GET HERE?

When Mother Teresa died, the media reported that she left behind only a bed, a chair, and a blue sweater. Your reaction is (a) How wonderful to be so focused, to have only what you need and nothing more! (b) That's all well and good, but *I* could never live that way, or (c) How did she ever manage without a PalmPilot?

Though many of us fantasize about traveling around the world, carefree, with everything we own in one suitcase, our real lives and our relationship to our "stuff" is far more complicated. A bag lady can fit everything she owns into a shopping cart and travel light, but most of us are secretly afraid of ending up that way. We calm our fears by acquiring a cushion of possessions to reassure ourselves and other people that that won't happen.

We also live in a country where it seems un-American not to have more things than we can keep track of, a society in which the largest homes, automobiles, or cheeseburgers are believed to be the best. Our instinct to accumulate has deep roots. Our parents or grandparents, in the shadow of the Depression, learned to keep an iron grip on anything that might still have some "good" in it. Little got thrown away. Then in the postwar 1940s and 1950s, Americans were encouraged to "Buy, buy, buy!" and to acquire every luxury they could afford. An anonymous government film from the late 1940s extols "the pleasure of buying, the spending of money! And the enjoyment of all the things that paychecks can buy are making happy all the thousands of families!"

Awkward grammar aside, from patriotic spending, we segued into a society in which items began being manufactured so cheaply that when you couldn't find the one you owned, you just bought another. The Reagan years popularized visible consumption by the wealthiest Americans. The Joneses that our parents were encouraged to keep up with were left in the dust; the introduction of upscale advertisements, Horchow catalogs, and *Lifestyles of the Rich and Famous* showed what abundant living actually meant. Now, instead of just the Joneses, we started comparing ourselves with millionaires.

THE CROWDED PRESENT

Even if you feel that does not describe you, you are probably bobbing around in a sea of too much stuff. A sociologist friend has the theory that people spend the first 40 years of their life enthusiastically accumulating and the next 40 years trying to get rid of the excess. That makes sense. As young adults, we start out with little but old term papers and cute stuffed animals. We quickly acquire cast-off furniture and household accessories donated by family members and friends, gratefully accepting anything free. Weddings generate gifts, often in multiples, sometimes items we didn't even realize existed. An electric bagel cutter—who knew?

Once we have a place to live, we head for our stores of choice, Ikea or Pottery Barn or Target, and purchase everything else we have been told we have to have. Credit cards make it easy to buy everything at once. And so we keep on accumulating until, one day, we realize that we have been buried alive, that too much of our time is spent managing stuff or just trying to find it. It may not be until a major life change such as moving forces us to take action.

Once in a while, a wake-up call comes sooner. Judi's came when she was in her early thirties and spent a week at the beach in a vacation house. The kitchen contained only the essentials that were needed to make easy meals; the living room and bedroom could be straightened up in a matter of minutes, leaving the family free to relax and explore for the rest of the day. For the first time in her life, she knew exactly where everything was. The experience was an epiphany. She came home determined to have that "vacation house feeling" for the rest of her life.

GETTING THE VACATION HOUSE FEELING

Unlike Marj, who was organizing her aunt's cupboards at 9 years old—and whose numerous moves as an adult kept her from excessive accumulation—Judi was a disaster. She was an artist and writer whose materials were everywhere, a collector of memorabilia and injured furniture that she planned to turn into "antiques." Her husband, Tom, stockpiled music and photography magazines as well as the gadgets that went with them. Her son had the full gamut of toys and school papers. Worst of all, her mother was a professional shopper; at holidays, her family was inundated with clothing and antiques.

And those were just the *personal* complications, added to the pressure of abundance as the way to show that you were a respectable American. Judi's parents had come of age during the Depression and passed along its characteristic sense of responsibility for everything that crossed your path, down to the fat red rubber bands that held the stalks of broccoli together and were "too good" to throw away. The rubber bands joined the little packets of soy sauce, free coupon books, and mystery screws as protected species.

Judi did manage to get that vacation house feeling, but it took her years to unlearn a lifestyle she had accepted without question. Scaling down meant looking at everything she owned—an enormous task—and deciding whether it should go or stay. She had to face her fears and learn to say no. It is an ongoing process. When she recently bought a laptop computer so that she could write while away from home, the saleswoman informed her that not only was she eligible for a free memory upgrade (which she needed) but that an ink-jet printer was part of the package. By the time she mailed in the rebates, the woman continued brightly, the printer would cost her nothing.

Judi considered it, then said no. She already had a more expensive ink jet printer and didn't want the complications of rebate coupons and storing the printer until a beneficiary was found.

"But it was free!" a friend protested. "Why not just take it?"

Why not? Because it was not actually "free." It came loaded with complications—needing storage room, needing a permanent home, needing several kinds of paperwork completed. And the longer something stays in a place "temporarily," the less likely it is to ever leave.

This is the background against which you will be working as you try to scale down and keep or buy only what is meaningful to you. It will mean continuing to say no to what you don't need, while making decisions about what is already there. It will mean understanding what your blind spots are before you start.

IDENTIFYING "STICKY" CLUTTER

Blind spots are called that for a reason; often people think that it is just a matter of getting started and straightforwardly paring down their belongings. That works, but only until you hit an area that feels uncomfortable and causes you to abandon the whole simplifying project. If you feel that you don't have any quirks about "stuff," check to see if you still own any of the following:

- Appliances, computer equipment, stereo systems, or televisions that have been replaced by ones that work better or have more features. But you're holding onto the original just in case the new replacement breaks down.

- Gifts or artwork from family or friends that you feel you have to display or at least keep because you are afraid the giver will be upset if you don't. How about all those inherited items, such as multiple sets of china you never use? You don't use them because you don't like them or prefer the dishes you bought yourself.

- Inoffensive duplicates such as collapsible umbrellas. Why *not* have six or seven? What if one breaks, or you want to lend one to visitors during an unexpected deluge? What kind of weird person would have only one collapsible umbrella?

- Teaching materials, engineering manuals, or any kind of vocational papers for a job you no longer have and to which you never plan to return. How about college textbooks, notes, and research papers or other items from your school years you will probably never look at again?

- Items that were free—a donation, raffle prize, or curbside find—that make you feel ahead of the game. Discarding them feels as though you are giving up your advantage.

- Shoes that hurt your feet but still look new.

- A collection that isn't yet complete because you've lost interest in it.

- Juicers, foreign-language tapes, exercise equipment, craft materials, or anything else you purchased and never really used—but which you hope to use in the future, so the acquisition won't prove to have been a mistake.

- Stacks of magazines still waiting for you to read "the good stuff" or being kept for reference. In the back of your mind, do you have the universal fear that if you throw away unread newspapers, magazines, and catalogs, you'll miss the one magic answer that you need to improve your life?

- Cartons of stuff you can't get rid of because they aren't yours. They belong to your adult children who say they want them but "don't have room" to take them now, or belong to parents or other relatives who are in assisted living and will never need them again.

And these aren't even the serious things that you will need to make decisions about. There's no question that "stuff" is sticky, and our defenses are high. A woman in one of our workshops quoted her father as saying, "If you don't have to feed it or bathe it or send it to college, what's the harm in keeping it?" The harm, if you have lived in your house for 40 years or even in your apartment for 5, is that things that don't demand any special care can still create clutter, take up valuable space, and fail to add anything to your sense of well-being. Even if they have not been a problem before, now that you are moving to a different space or streamlining your life, they are among the things that will need to go.

HOW STUFFED ARE YOU?

When we give our workshops, we usually start with a short quiz so that people can determine whether or not they are in the right seminar. It also helps to set the mood.

1. Do you feel as if you have too much "stuff" in your life?
2. Is your car trunk too full to find the spare tire? Is your garage too full to fit the car inside?
3. Are you holding on to magazines and newspapers to read "the good stuff"? Is the pile growing?
4. Do you feel responsible for items you never asked to own—the fat red rubber bands from around broccoli stalks, angel pins, address labels, calendars, and other "gifts" from charities, heavy plastic wonton soup containers and little packets of soy sauce, used bows and wrapping paper from gifts you've been given?
5. Do you have direction booklets and warranties for appliances you no longer own?
6. Are you keeping books you "couldn't get into" with the idea that someday maybe you'll be able to finish them?
7. Do you believe that broken appliances stored in a basement or garage can heal themselves?
8. Have you ever bought a duplicate item because you could not find the one you knew you had?
9. Do people give you theme collectibles (e.g., ceramic frogs, cats, Precious Moment figurines) that you're no longer interested in, but feel you must display because they were gifts?
10. Do you have cartons of books, college papers, wedding gifts, or family heirlooms that you haven't looked at for 5 years or more?
11. Have the same papers been sitting on your desk for more than 3 weeks?
12. Do you have clothes that you can't wear because they are permanently stained, need to be hemmed or mended, or have suddenly somehow become miniscule?

13. Is your basement or garage a repository of scraps of wood, tile, linoleum, wallpaper, and nearly empty paint cans from old projects that you think you might need someday for touch-ups?

14. Are there more than 100 catalogs in your home right now?

15. Do you keep all the cartons your appliances and computer equipment came in "in case you have to ship them back"?

16. Are you afraid if you dispose of those mystery screws, odd metal parts, and other bits you can't identify that something terrible will happen?

If you've answered four or more of these questions with "Yes," you're reading the right book.

IS BIGGER BETTER?

There is a pervasive prejudice in our culture that more is preferable. That building up is inherently better than scaling down. Think about all the restaurant menus that tell you that you are getting a 16-ounce steak, and they have two sizes of prime rib; what real man would order the Queen cut? It is the same mentality that assumes that moving to a smaller place is a step downward, that having fewer luxuries makes you appear less successful as a person. Perhaps it is enough to recognize that this attitude exists but that it has started acquiring some resistance. The more inner-directed and grounded you are in yourself, the less such opinions will matter to you. When you think about it objectively, the notion that some people are judging your worth by the things you own, rather than by your personality and achievements, seems absurd.

The other thing to recognize is that scaling down does not mean renouncing your own style. It is actually a heightening of focus on the things you love and that reflect your essence. It means stripping away the clutter of whatever no longer fits or does not contribute to making your life easier—and by "easier," we don't mean having every laborsaving gadget. We are talking about the ability to look in a drawer and find a potato peeler or hammer or an airplane ticket immediately. Living the life you want may mean looking for amenities in a new place that you don't have now or remodeling your current home to reflect who you truly are.

To scale down in a way that makes your life richer, you will need a mission statement.

THE MISSION STATEMENT

Whenever we go to someone's home to save them from drowning in debris, the first thing we do is sit down, usually over coffee, and talk about what they want to accomplish. Each situation is different, and each client has different priorities. We may be called on to rearrange furniture, evaluate wardrobes, or bring order to shopping bags full of papers. By the time we are called to the scene, people have either gone as far as they are able to on their own or recognize that they don't have the time or motivation to do it themselves. Sometimes—half in dread and half in hope—they expect us to sweep in like Queer Eye for the Straight Guy's Fab Five and just make everything disappear.

We don't, of course. If you've ever gone into your parents' home and started trying to throw away "clutter" or had someone say to you, "Why are you keeping *that* old thing?" you know that nothing is more personal than our stuff. Many times our clientele have some idea of what they want to have happen, but if they haven't thought about specifics, we do so together. Marj gives her clients a preliminary list of questions to answer, such as "Name your biggest limitation—budget, time, or space?" and has them identify for themselves their specific problem areas.

When Judi began her own personal decluttering, her mission statement was "I want to have that vacation house feeling. So I will need to pare down to only what's necessary or very special." She might also have put it, "I'm tired of being a household drudge, feeling resentful when I do take time to clean and guilty when I don't. So I will have only as many things as I can easily handle." Through the ups and downs of the journey, this goal was the light at the end of the clutter.

Distilling Your Purpose

If you are reading this book, chances are you already have an idea of what you want to accomplish. But you will need to put that feeling into words. Distilling your purpose into a sentence helps to crystallize where you are going and gives you a sense of direction. We call this your Scaling Down Mission Statement. It will help when things seem overwhelming, as they will. When you are plopped on the floor surrounded by boxes of old photographs of people you can't identify and wonder, "Why in God's name am I doing this?" you will have an answer.

Here are some of the mission statements of people with whom we have worked:

- I want to turn the garage from hell into an office for a part-time financial consulting business. So I will need to clear out all the junk and furnish the room in a way that gives me confidence and makes my clients feel secure about my abilities.

- I need to help my parents move into assisted living without too much trauma. So I will help them take the best with them and find good homes for everything else.

- We're selling our house and have picked out a great apartment in the city. So we have to sort through 40 years of stuff and take only what we need in our new life.

- I want to create an attractive guest room and invite company without agonizing about it. So I will find a permanent home for everything that is stored in there now and keep it from creeping back.

- We're getting married and have to merge two cluttered apartments into one space. So we will focus on the kind of life we really want rather than just jamming in what we already have.

- I need to organize a lifetime of memorabilia and photographs into some kind of meaningful order. So I will gather it all in one place and get rid of everything that doesn't matter. My children will thank me!

- I want my home to represent me, with room for new energy and experiences to come into my life. So I will get rid of things that keep me stuck in the past and replace them with what is important to me now.

When we were formulating a mission statement for this book, we arrived at the following: "We want to help people assess the quantity and meaning of stuff in their lives—especially if they have to move or want to fulfill personal goals—and come to a happy and manageable solution." The word "stuff" uses the dictionary meaning of "household or personal articles collectively; belongings. Worthless objects; refuse or junk."

You may find you have several goals that you can list sequentially. Or you may find it hard to construct even one sentence. In that case, start out by jotting down a few key words, and go from there. Some words and phrases that come to mind are: compact, defining me as an individual, cozy, things I love, decluttered, entertaining more, only what I need, easy living, Feng Shui, room to do art, home office, being in control, feeling closer to nature, and so on. Get out a clean sheet of paper, and write down all of your goals for scaling down or the words that come to mind in your vision of what you want when you complete this process.

Then begin on your Scaling Down Mission Statement. Structure it as follows:

*I need to*_____

_____

_____

So I will _____

_____

_____

It's okay to have several "I need to" and "So I will" statements in your mission statement. But try to combine or pare them down to a concise summary of what's most important to you.

When Words Won't Come

If you have trouble putting together your Scaling Down Mission Statement, recognize what you're really doing here is identifying and articulating your own feelings. You may believe that you are in a situation where you have no choice but to go forward and have a lot of inner resistance as a result. Suppose you have to clear out your parents' house so that it can be sold, but you keep putting it off. In that case, you may want to use a somewhat different approach. Write the first part of your mission statement, and then create a second paragraph for your "Buts." For example . . .

I need to clean out my parents' house.
BUT I hate it that they can no longer live there.
BUT I know going through the stuff will bring up a lot of memories for me.
BUT with a full-time job, I don't have time to do it.
BUT I don't know what to do with all the stuff.

I need to _____

_____

_____

BUT _____

_____

_____

BUT _____

_____

_____

BUT _____

_____

_____

After you have written out your objections, think about ways you can address them. Even if it is something you can do nothing about, such as the inevitable passage of time, your regret is a valid feeling and needs to be recognized. As for the second "But," do you have to face your memories alone? Maybe you have siblings or cousins or friends who can spend a weekend working with you, turning it into a time of reminiscing; they may have some ideas of how to handle the job that you have not thought of. It would also help with the third area of not having enough time, if you could get the bulk of the clearing out done in a weekend and take things such as papers and photographs home with you to sort at your leisure. If there is absolutely no one to work with you, and you live out of state, you may want to hire a declutterer to do all but the fine-tuning.

Your Scaling Down Mission Statement may now read, "I need to clean out my parents' house with support and help. So I will ask _____ to work with me."

As far as not knowing what to do with the stuff, that's where we can help. One reason we wrote this book was to explain the many options you have and the specific places to which you can make donations rather than simply throwing things away.

SEEING VISIONS

When you are scaling down your own home or planning new areas, it can help to have a photograph of what you want, clipped from a magazine or scanned from a book. Tape it up where you will see it regularly. Having a photo of a beautiful home office will help you create one. Images have a powerful effect on the subconscious. A mental picture you create yourself will do as well. Sometimes at the end of our workshops, we ask people to close their eyes, relax, and visualize a change they want to make—whether it's a beautifully clean desk, a transformed basement, or a living room filled only with what they love.

Once they have the picture clearly in mind, we explain that if they focus on it every night before sleep or every morning on waking for about a week, it will become a reality. When you give your subconscious an idea, your mind begins to work on how to create it. You will be focused in that direction and start getting things done.

While we're on the subject of motivation, which is what having a mission statement is about, it helps to remember a technique Judi uses: "Action comes before motivation." In other words, there are certain things such as exercising, cleaning bathrooms, or sorting through stacks of clothing that most people are not highly motivated to do. But if you are familiar with exercise, you know that once you have been walking or doing aerobics for about 15 minutes, your motivation kicks in, and you start enjoying it. The same is true with organizing and creating a new space. It may seem too overwhelming to even begin, a hopeless job requiring more energy than you will ever have. But if you set a timer for 15 minutes and dive in, promising yourself that you can stop when the buzzer goes off, you'll be surprised—both at the amount you have been able to achieve and that you are now in the spirit of it and don't want to stop.

Action comes before motivation.

A CAUTIONARY TALE

In case you're still not convinced of the benefits of a having a Scaling Down Mission Statement, here is an example of a couple who did not have one. This is how Judi tells it:

"Mary Alice, a lovely woman in her early seventies, called me one day to say that she and her husband, George, had attended my workshop 2 years earlier and had finally found the handout with my phone number. They needed my help with a clutter problem. The misplaced phone number might have been a tip-off; the small window in the front door taped over with cardboard definitely was.

"I had been told to come to the side door, and Mary Alice brought me in through an enclosed porch. It was stacked to the ceiling with cartons, tools, and lawn furniture. Once we were inside, we could get past the kitchen, but reaching the table would have been physically impossible. Instead, we talked in the hallway. When I tried to find out what their priorities were, Mary Alice and George looked vague: 'My son thinks we need to clear out some stuff,' George said finally, chuckling.

"After a tour of the downstairs and a look at a bathtub that was stacked high with dishes in cartons, unused photo albums, and old shoes, I suggested that our first goal might be to clear a path through the living room. They quickly agreed. But that was *my* mission statement, not theirs. Everything I unearthed was either greeted with happy surprise—'I wondered where that was!'—or designated to be donated for raffle to a particular charity. Many of the things I uncovered, in fact, had been door prizes from the many organizations to which they belonged.

Since there was no clear space in the house to put the donations, they had to stay stacked with everything else, facing the clear probability that they would disappear back into the clutter once I had gone.

"Four hours later, I had managed to collect only one brown grocery bag filled with trash, the only items with which they were willing to part. We had created a narrow walkway through the living room but, like the parting of the Red Sea, I was certain it would soon be covered over. Seeing how exhausted George and Mary Alice were, I suggested quitting for the day. Actually, I told them I would come back only when they were ready to make a plan that we could follow.

"We parted amicably. I haven't heard from them."

If you're sure that you have no ambivalence about scaling down, you can skip Chapter 2 and get started. Otherwise, it's time to take a look at some of the fears and blind spots you may not have even realized were there.

2

I NEED TO DO THIS BUT . . .

In one of our workshops, "Lose 40 Pounds Overnight: The New Decluttering Diet," an attractive young woman raised her hand just before we began. "You're going to give us the magic answer to making everything spacious and uncluttered—aren't you?"

We laughed and told her, "No magic bullet, but we can tell you one thing that *would* work. If you were to do it, you wouldn't even need to stay for the rest of the program."

By now the whole group was listening.

"All you need to do is go home and get rid of exactly half of the things you have. Clothes, kitchenware, collectibles, everything. Save the best, and get rid of everything else. You'll still have plenty, and you won't have a clutter problem."

They looked as if we had told them to go home and murder their favorite pet. No one got up and left to do it.

But that was not a surprise. People's relationships with the things they have accumulated are so complex that it is difficult to imagine anyone going home and blithely tossing out half their world. What most people want is a quick and painless answer, a magic bullet that can be shot once into the clutter, leaving their home—once the dust clears—in perfect order. And without stirring up any messy emotions, of course.

We understand how they feel. The bad news is that there is no magic bullet; if there were, *we* would know about it. The good news is that once you face the ambivalence you have about scaling down, once you create a mission statement and actually get started, you will feel better and better. Part of it will be catharsis, and part of it will grow out of your sense of decisiveness and gaining control, a sense that you are moving into the next adventure of your life. If we had an empty trash bag for everyone who has said, "I should have done this years ago!" we would be able to declutter the East Coast.

Scaling down is not that different from physically traveling to an unknown place. You may have a profound fear of flying—or just the usual uneasiness that makes it necessary for you to concentrate on keeping the plane airborne. But the more flights you take, the more times you safely reach your destination and have a wonderful time, the less ambivalence you'll have about your next plane trip. Some people find that their apprehension never entirely leaves them; others start feeling cranky if they have to be in the vicinity of an airport without being able to board a plane themselves.

THE GREAT FEARS OF SCALING DOWN

Unlike the fear of flying, where the main focus is on whether or not the plane will stay in the air and actually land where it should, fears of scaling down are more varied. These are the top 21 apprehensions that we've come across in our practice:

1. I'll make a mistake and get rid of things I might need later on.
We've all had the experience of discarding an item and then deciding a week later that we could have used it after all. On the other hand, if you think hard enough, you can decide that every possession has some potential use and have an excuse to not get rid of anything. The kicker is that when the time comes that you could actually use it, either you will have forgotten you have it or not be able to find the item, buried as it will be in the clutter.

This is an area where you need to play the odds. If you have not used something in 5 years, the chances are remote that you will ever use it for anything—except, perhaps, to sabotage your mission statement.

If you feel you *have* to hold on to mystery screws and unfamiliar pieces of metal, at least put them together in a glass jar, so they can keep each other company, and you will know where to find them.

2. I won't be accepted by people if I scale down too drastically.

It depends on who you mean by "people." If, due to divorce, reduced income, or simply your own choice, you move from a large house to an apartment in a less-exclusive area, you may find that you have little in common with your former neighbors. Money and size have a large place in the minds of people who define themselves by what they own, people who need physical cues as to whom their friends should be. What you have done may threaten their own stability, and they may handle it by deciding you are no longer "one of us." Yes, certain people may be decluttered. Without shared interests, you may end up, after scaling down, with the friends to whom you relate on a truer level.

Two of Marj's clients, Lily and John, lived in a large house filled with artwork. People loved to come to their home, a gracious and beautiful spot with an outdoor patio that could accommodate 40 to 50 guests. Both of them loved to entertain. But they were in their early eighties and felt that the bi-level home and gardens were too much to keep up. Still, the idea of the whole process and how they would feel afterward in a condo "loomed like the Rockies" in their minds.

What they came to realize was that although they were scaling down, they would not be giving up the *essence* of who they were. Marj helped them see that they could select the best of what they owned and remain themselves. Even though they were sacrificing space, the ambiance was retained. Granted, there were some pangs of loss in the adjustment, but they lost no friends. "It's wonderful! Nothing looks missing," Lily said enthusiastically. "And we feel so much freer."

Whatever setting you are in, you can still be yourself.

3. It will be too painful to revisit certain parts of my life.

As always, you have choices. There is no rule that says you cannot take that group of cartons you have been hauling around with you from home to home and put them, unopened, in the trash. If you feel that it would be too painful to wade through reminders of hurtful relationships, happiness now vanished, opportunities not taken, then discard the cartons with our blessing. Making a clean sweep is preferable to doing nothing and letting the past continue to haunt you.

But consider the alternative of going through the boxes with a family member or friend. That way you will be able to talk, react, and have someone there to recognize the validity of your experiences and your feelings. For years, Marj carried with her the boxes that held memorabilia from her late husband and son who had both died young, including the cards, telegrams, and other papers from their memorial services.

When she felt it was time, she and her daughter, Angelyn, went through the cartons to see what was there and to choose what symbolic items they wanted to keep. They laughed and cried and hugged, and by the end, there had been catharsis and closure.

You can also go through emotion-laden materials with a specific purpose, such as to collect items for a Life Book (Chapter 12). In doing so, you can save what you want to remember and be remembered for and let go of the rest.

4. I'll get started and won't be able to follow through. I've begun so many other projects and abandoned them that I'm afraid the same thing will happen here.
Yes, it can happen, but it is far less likely to if you have your Scaling Down Mission Statement and a clear idea of what you want the end result to be. The real danger is in *not* having a clear goal to keep you focused. Over the years, we have seen people start to scale down in the initial flush of enthusiasm, get their home to a more manageable state, then taper off. One magazine at a time, clutter sneaks back in. You may read a decluttering book or take a workshop on organizing and come home as determined to clean out your garage as Carrie Nation storming her first saloon. You start off the day with enthusiasm, but since you don't have a clear plan or an image of what you want to accomplish, after a while, you will find yourself stymied by stacks of old tires, non-working bicycles, and the greasy cement floor. Suddenly cleaning out the garage seems an impossible job, and you quit "for now." And leave it alone until the next time you feel temporarily fired up.

This is where having a strong mission statement will get you through. Whether your written goal is "To clear out the garage, so we can sell the house" or "To clear out the garage, so I can have a potting bench and a gardening area and room for the car," if you have a visual image, it will help you keep going. Knowing that the tires and the broken bikes aren't part of your plan, you will research where you can get rid of them instead of giving up.

5. When I look at my surroundings and think about scaling down, there is so much stuff that I feel paralyzed. The idea of making decisions about everything is exhausting.

We know the feeling. We have been in homes far worse than you can imagine, places where there was not even a pathway to get through the stuff. Places where the piles teetered above our heads, where the file cabinets were so stuffed you could not pull *anything* out. We were there because their owners had shuddered and given up. Our task was to help them break through the paralysis and reclaim their space. Since you are trying to do it on your own, here are some techniques:

Start anywhere. In this book, we give you step-by-step instructions on how to attack a room, but sometimes you may feel too overwhelmed to follow them or even to create a mission statement. You need to just make a start—anywhere. Begin with what looks easy. Marla Cilley, the "Flylady" and author of the book *Sink Reflections* has what she calls "the 27-Fling Boogie" in which you take a plastic bag and move through the house, tossing out 27 items you can get rid of without much thought. (If you would like step-by-step guidance, her Web site is www.flylady.com.)

Just do it. Don't worry about whether you are doing it the "right way," whether or not you have the right storage containers, when the next garbage pickup is. It's easy to obsess and let perfectionism halt the process. *Just get started.*

Start with the areas you see all the time. We tell people to go for what will give the biggest bang for their buck, such as with Marj's client Charles, who dreaded walking through his apartment door. The first thing he saw was stuff piled on every living room chair—it seemed to give the message that no one else was welcome to come in and sit down. That was *his* place to start, an area that bothered him and was noticeable to everyone who came to the door. Pick a visual area such as an entrance hall or bookcase and work on it without getting sidetracked into other areas. You need to be able to see some difference.

Choose the best time of day. Mornings work well for most people, though others get their second wind at night. But things always seem worse and more hopeless when you're tired and haven't the energy to do anything about them. Get a good night's sleep, and face the impossible in the morning.

If the task seems too overwhelming, just leave. Take a notebook with you, and go out for a cup of coffee, diet cola, beer, glass of wine—any beverage of choice. Then mentally go through your home room by room, writing down what you need to discard, what you want to keep, what needs to be replaced. By writing things down, you are already getting some psychological distance from your things and imposing some order on what seems totally chaotic. Putting things down on paper is a strong motivator. If you write, "Get rid of that old stack of newspapers in the bedroom corner," you're a lot more likely to go home and put them by the curb to recycle them than if you just stare at them, shudder, and close the door.

6. I won't be able to "let go." Even though I think I can, when I actually start, it will be too hard.
Perhaps when you tried to do this in the past, you hit a roadblock and let it stop you. Or maybe you haven't yet tried—you haven't had to—and are guessing at how you will feel. But now that you are moving, scaling down, or setting new priorities, you have to at least give it a try. The only way to know what will happen is to actually begin.

Start with an area you know will be easy; when you are successful, you will feel more confident that you can continue to let things go. Loretta, a woman in our workshops, had "inherited" a complete set of baking tins from her mother-in-law's kitchen and also had many special pans she had collected over the years herself. Although she no longer had any interest in baking, and her husband had espoused a low-carbohydrate diet, she felt she wouldn't be able to give the collection up.

To her surprise, she found that it felt wonderfully freeing. She gave away muffin tins, cake pans, and frosting tips, everything but one cookie sheet that she used for grilling fish. "Nobody needs more carbs," she said. "And right in town, we have a great bakery for emergencies."

You don't have to give everything away at once. If you have to, take it in stages, and see how letting go feels. In most cases, the fear of letting go is worse than the actuality.

7. I'm happy just as I am. Why do I have to change?

If you don't have to move to another space and if being a pack rat gives you joy and doesn't interfere with your relationships, then go for it. Maybe someone who doesn't understand your true nature gave you this book by mistake.

Judi's father would have been unmoved by such a book. He was very happy to squirrel things away and never discarded anything he felt was "good." He had a large house and basement, a backyard shed, and rental space. After he died, it was a treasure hunt for his children, discovering his Eagle Scout award sandwiched in with utility bills that had been paid 20 years earlier and letters home from World War II. But it took them weeks to sort through it all, and they filled a large dumpster just by clearing out the garage and half the basement.

You may think that your children or younger relatives will also enjoy the treasure hunt. But maybe they won't. Your treasures may end up being trashed without even being sorted. If you are going to bequeath everything you've come across to your heirs, make sure you have what is important labeled.

We find that people who aren't convinced that there's any payoff to changing their behaviors won't do it. But a word about not changing: Even if you're a happy pack rat, consider the idea that by making physical space around you, you are opening the door for new experiences to come in.

8. I'm not giving up all my stuff as long as he/she holds on to his/hers.

Ask yourself: Am I really afraid I will have no presence in the house if I scale down my own things? Or is this a convenient way for both of us to stay stuck and not have to move—physically or emotionally? "If he can keep all his model railroading magazines, I can have 20 years of December decorating issues." And so everyone gets the chance to keep their clutter without taking action. If it really is a standoff about things, you may need to have an outsider, an objective organizer or counselor, come in and arbitrate.

But there are good reasons why you should scale down your own belongings, even though your partner refuses to touch his or hers. When people are proactive with their stuff, it often inspires their spouses to start in on theirs, especially when they see how much easier it makes life. They may at least back off from the impasse. Scaling down isn't about stripping yourself of your identity and comforts. And though you wish it could be otherwise, the only person you can control is yourself.

9. I have too many _____, but I have no clear favorites. Everything is "good enough," but nothing stands out.

Are you afraid that if you scale down, you'll be left with a few mediocre things instead of a lot of them? Is it a matter of not knowing what to get rid of since nothing stands out as a keeper? A lot of things that are useful are not especially thrilling. But even with something as prosaic as a hammer, if you have several, there is probably one that feels more comfortable to hold and that is heavy enough to do most household repairs. You may not love the one you keep, but once it is chosen, you will be able to let go of the others you've amassed over the years.

What we're saying is that the choice may seem arbitrary or marginal. But it still needs to be made. The best option is to replace six mediocre items with one that you love, though that is not always financially possible. We don't agree with the idea that buying something new is "wasteful" and that you should be sentenced forever to something ugly just because you now own it.

This is especially true with clothes. When we discuss clothing in our workshops, we advise people that before they discard anything, they should select three or four outfits that they wear regularly and feel comfortable and attractive in. In order to put together these outfits, you may need to add a few items. But once you are confident that you have something appropriate to wear, it is much easier to give away clothing that no longer fits or that you just don't like.

10. My things are part of me.

Yes, it is easy for certain belongings to get overpersonalized and take on a life of their own. We begin to see our things as an extension of ourselves, as if they are somehow alive. We fall into the magic thinking that they will feel hurt and rejected if we discard them. Judi learned that lesson the hard way years ago when she was helping her 11-year-old son go through his dresser drawers. When he placed a rolled-up pair of navy blue socks he had never worn on the giveaway pile, she picked them up and teased, "Oh, Andy, don't you *like* us? We've been waiting here day after day. How can you just give us away?" He snatched back the socks and insisted on keeping them—though he still never wore them.

But socks don't have personalities or feelings any more than cars or couch pillows or briefcases, especially if they are mass-produced. We may consider that they are a part of us, but they have no awareness of it. Pets have personalities; toy teddy bears don't, even though we may give them names and cute characteristics. Parents often start this trend inadvertently by personalizing stuffed animals and acting as if they are alive. If you have leanings in this direction, when you discard something, practice saying, "You helped me, and I'm grateful, but I know *you're* not feeling anything right now."

11. I feel like I'll be throwing away my history.

This is a sticking point for many people. We feel we need playbills, birthday cards, term papers, and other visual cues to remind us of our past. It is external proof that we have lived in a particular way and been happy. There is nothing wrong with saving memorabilia if the items are confined to one box. Later in the book, we discuss other methods of preserving memories such as saving a representative or taking a photograph. In the meantime, it is helpful to ask yourself "If I want to look ahead and experience each new day, why do I need to recall my past in detail?" That collection of specialty diet books and recipes may be part of your history, but why keep them around when none of them worked?

12. It seems disrespectful to get rid of *any* of my grandparents'/parents' things.

We will discuss how to sort through family belongings in "Clearing Out Your Family Home," but to get started on your mission to scale down now, simply remind yourself that stuff is, ultimately, just stuff. Much of what you have in cartons from your parents' home was not sacred to them. A beloved pocket watch has a different value from an old baking tin, even though both may have dents. Going through family items can be a slow process and usually one that has to be repeated several times. First of all, pick out several items that you love and remind you of the essence of the person. If you have children, ask them to pick out something they want. Then select some items from the lower end of the spectrum and donate them. It is not disrespectful if your family's things can bless someone else.

13. A lot of stuff belongs to my adult children who don't have room to take the things. I can't just throw them away.

If you are giving your children free storage, there's no reason for them to even think about "making room." Why should they? It may not have been a problem for you before, but if you are moving to a more compact space or have designs on that room or closet, you will need to get tough. Some parents give children a deadline to sort and take their belongings or, if they are at a distance, box the items up and ship them. Others take the time to cull through old school papers and artwork and put the best of them in albums.

But be prepared to find that you may be more attached to their things than they are. Last year, Judi went through her son's childhood artwork and framed one of the pieces to give to him for Christmas. His wife liked it; he did not remember making it at all.

There may be larger pieces of furniture and heirlooms that your children want, but truly have no room to keep in a studio apartment. In that case, a small storage bin, reasonably priced, is the best option. Be careful about asking anyone else to keep furniture for you "temporarily."

When Louise, a friend of Judi's parents, moved to New York from France, she "lent" a beautiful antique couch to a married couple who had a large house. By the time Louise had room to take the couch 13 years later and tracked down her friends who were now living in another state, they had already had the wood refinished and the fabric reupholstered and had no intention of giving it back.

Even if people are willing to return a piece of furniture, it may not be in the same condition as when it was entrusted to their care. Or, they may have forgotten to whom it belonged and sold it at their last garage sale.

14. My things are an outward expression of who I am.

For some people, home is where they eat and sleep and take showers. For others, it is a reflection of who they are, their personalities made visible. Each room has been furnished with love and care. While you do not feel that things are necessary to make you a complete person, you enjoy having them around you. You may not feel that you can give up *anything*.

Yet there is a subtle difference between things to which you are personally attached and the things that you feel demonstrate you are creative, discerning, and humane, a person of wit and good taste. Or that you are a serious scholar, to which your 10 shelves of volumes on paleontology attest. But do you still use them all—or are many of them kept for "show"? As we discussed earlier, scaling down does not mean giving up the essence of who you are. But think about this: Even if you no longer owned a single book, piece of artwork or funny motto, people would still have a very good idea of who you were.

15. Nobody wants my things, and I'm not just going to throw them in the trash!

Human nature being what it is, it's easier to make that kind of blanket statement and stay where you are, rather than look at items individually and find homes for them. It's true that many charities do not want threadbare furnishings, nonfunctioning appliances, or faded clothes and textiles. But part of the purpose of this book is to show how you can find places even for outdated clothing and accessories, old suitcases, books, and broken electronics. If this is why you are having trouble making a mission statement, look at the chapter called "Finding Good Homes."

16. The old-fashioned virtue of "Waste not, want not" was instilled in me. How can I get rid of things that have no resale value but are still "perfectly good"?

Ah, refrigerator magnets from local businesses, those attractive, empty olive oil bottles, plastic shopping bags, sturdy Chinese take-out containers. And their cousins: birthday candles that were only used once but announce it when you put them on a fresh cake, the painkiller the dentist prescribed that still has a few tablets left in the cylinder, the wrapping paper you carefully saved despite its telltale folds and white creases.

Start by setting limits on the "perfectly good." That is, keep five rubber bands and eight frozen dinner containers if you know you can use them, and recycle the others. Say no to condiments you won't use up, and toss mailed items such as coupons, calendars, return address labels printed with your name, and other charitable enticements. Don't even open the envelope.

As far as their cousins are concerned, the gently used, if you have an understanding with family and friends that you will recycle wrapping paper or candles, that's fine. But be aware that people take a jaundiced view of receiving Christmas cards with the original sender's name covered over and yours written in.

A cautionary tale: When New York playwright Laura's golden retriever, Scout, was very ill, the vet sold her some ground organic turkey to feed him. Sadly, Scout died soon after, and Laura was left with 5 pounds of expensive frozen meat.

Granted, there were bones and sinew ground up in it, but that did not stop her from planning turkey loaf and turkey burger dinners. At the first meal, when her family realized what they were eating, they rebelled. Laura reluctantly gave the remainder to another friend with a dog.

Everything "perfectly good" does not have to be kept and used.

17. Some things are just too charming to give away.

Friends of ours have a pillow with Mona Lisa's portrait, which giggles every time you touch it. It is funny when an unsuspecting person leans against it, then jumps, startled at the sound of the sofa laughing at them. But eventually, it will lose its charm (or its squeaker) and have to be recycled. When you purchase novelty items, be aware that even the best of them are time limited. After a while, they won't amuse you anymore and will cease to be entertaining to your friends. The pillow that reads, "One spoiled bitch lives here" and the "Turtle Crossing" garden sign have done their job and should be passed on to someone else.

Even pieces of art that have more than novelty value can benefit from not being on display all the time.

18. I'm afraid if I cut way down, I won't have the freedom of choice I do now—what to wear, read, eat, watch on video.

Everyone who has actually watched every TV program they've taped "to watch later," raise your hand. You are excused. For most people, the problem is having too many choices and too little time. You have stacks of magazines you want to read "someday" and a closet full of clothing waiting to be chosen. But you wear your favorite clothes and play your favorite CDs over and over and rarely select anything from the other 80 percent. In essence, we stockpile things for a blizzard that never comes.

By contrast, imagine how freeing it would feel if every video, CD, book, clothing item, or food on your pantry shelf was something you enthusiastically wanted to use—and did use. Try to evaluate your collections on that basis, and you will find that you have cut down to manageable amounts.

19. It may sound silly, but I need to leave some physical evidence behind that I've been here.

There is nothing silly about the desire to be remembered, no matter what your belief or lack of belief in an afterlife. It is an area that deserves thought. What would you like to be remembered for? What aspect of your life do you want to pass on, other than your image in photographs and in your Life Book? For Judi, it is copies of the books she has written and a small collection of heirloom silver napkin rings. Mari wants her family to have her delicate bone china cups and saucers.

Once you think it through, you'll know what *not* to give away and can let a lot of other things go.

20. I'm so busy that I don't have time to stay home and scale down. Sure, I'd like to get things sorted out, but isn't it better to have a life?
Time—or lack of time—is everyone's problem, and setting priorities can be murky. But people who are so busy that they don't have a moment to catch their breath should stop long enough to consider what is going on. Plunging into a new project can be a lot more enjoyable than plunging into your basement. Being busy and overextended can make you feel valued by other people. Being "too busy to think" can keep you from having to make painful changes. Creating works of art and taking classes can give you the feeling of doing something meaningful the way sorting through junk mail can't.

The key is balance, not an either/or approach. Having a life means having one all the time, experiencing mindfulness in everything you do. If things are chaotic at home, you'll want to spend even less time there instead of using your space as a necessary retreat. As far as scaling down, you already know that stuffing things into cartons and leaving them for someone else to sort is not a good answer. While you don't have to cut out your "important" activities permanently, consider taking a break long enough to do a major paring down. You'll save time by not having to search for misplaced necessities and feel more serene and able to focus when you are home.

21. I hate making decisions. Period.
Except for a few movers and shakers who thrive on being decisive, the rest of us find making decisions exhausting. At the end of a typical day of decluttering, after we have left, our clients may continue for a little while, then crash. "I'm glad you told me what to expect," one woman said. "When I collapsed on the couch and didn't move all evening, I thought I was getting sick!"

That said, once you start making decisions about your stuff, the process becomes exhilarating and carries its own momentum. Most people have a "self improvement gene," and refining your belongings means making your world better. We'll be giving you specific techniques, such as triage and miniaturization, and ways to make the process easier. In general, it helps to start with something easy—obvious garbage—to build your confidence. It also helps to declutter when you are feeling cranky, since being in a bad mood tends to make people decisive. Or set a timer for 15 minutes, and tell yourself you'll stop at that point if making decisions still feels uncomfortable.

The important thing is to recognize that a dislike of making decisions is common to a lot of us, but that in this instance, there's a satisfying payoff as well.

If you are still feeling conflicted, it is time to grab a fresh sheet of paper and write a two-step mission statement. First, put down what your purpose is; then try to articulate what is holding you back. Complete this sentence:

I need to _____

Then list the obstacles that are making this transition difficult. Use this format:

But _____

_____

After you have thought it through, create a revised statement:

*I need to*_____

_____

_____

So I will _____

_____

_____

Besides helping you to stay focused on the outcome, your Scaling Down Mission Statement will help you plan how to get where you are going. If you know your destination, it is easier to figure out the route. The next few chapters will help you identify and overcome obstacles in your path.

part 2
THE CULPRITS

"Tag sale next door!"

3

BUT AUNT WINNIE GAVE IT TO ME!

It was time for audience questions, a favorite part of our workshops. A man who had been listening intently raised his hand. "I taught accounting for 30 years, and I still have all my materials. They're stored neatly in cartons, but my wife says they're cluttering up the basement." It was a familiar situation.

"How many cartons?"

"A few," he admitted. His wife, sitting next to him, rolled her eyes. In our experience, "a few" means 20 to 30. "But it's good stuff! It's the texts I used, important bulletins, lesson plans, stuff like that."

"Do you plan on going back to teaching?"

"No way. I love being retired. But I might want to look at the things sometime."

There is a category of belongings—career materials, a lifetime of artwork, beautiful calendars and periodicals, photographs, handmade and store-bought gifts—that can be difficult to scale down because of our own complicated feelings about what they represent as well as the individual items themselves. What makes it more difficult is that the materials don't have much monetary value or interest for other people, so they cannot be easily passed along. And, except for photographs, most aren't small enough to fit in a memorabilia box.

If you are like most Americans, at least one of these categories has taken up residence in your home or will attempt to in the future. Before we can evict any part of them, it is helpful to understand their emotional pull.

CAREER MATERIALS

If you have retired or changed jobs, chances are good that when you left, you cleared out your workspace by stowing everything in cartons—from your favorite coffee mug to a 20-year-old training manual and your wall calendar. You may have jettisoned some papers that were obviously trash and left behind files for your successor. But few people are able to seriously sort at that time or even know what they will want to save for the future. You probably also have a collection of goodbye cards, letters of appreciation, parting gifts, and photographs from the party.

Unless you are moving immediately, we suggest waiting about a year to go through this material. By then, you will be settled into your new life and routines and have some perspective on what was valuable about your work. You will have a better idea of whether or not you want to continue your expertise in some other form. If you decide to do so, it will be necessary to extract the appropriate materials and jettison the rest. But don't be surprised to find that most of the materials you need are in your head and not in boxes. Bear in mind also that your new activity will generate more materials, so you need to be firm about getting rid of now-obsolete papers.

A LIFETIME OF ART

Picasso made little sketches on the backs of checks, knowing that most of them would be framed and never cashed—a unique way to save money and sell art at the same time. But most artists, especially those who have done it as an avocation, don't have that option, and in fact, end up with a studio or a roomful of work. Most people are involved in some creative outlet, whether painting, pottery, photography, quilting, or woodworking, and have an inventory of pieces. You know you can't take them all with you when you move and might not want to keep them all if you could. But just throwing them away is unthinkable; the things you have created are literally a part of you.

While there is no perfect answer, there are certain steps you can take:

- Set a period of time aside to go through your work. Some pieces that you may have forgotten about will move you and make you marvel that *you* created them. Other pieces—experiments that didn't turn out, imitations of artists you admired early on, work in which you lost inspiration or couldn't quite get right—will make you wince. There is nothing wrong with discarding the second group. Don't fall into the "accurate record" trap. It is better to react like Phil, a Long Island artist, who looked through newsprint pads of life class drawings from his student

---

HOW TO TRULY LEAVE YOUR JOB BEHIND

Most people who leave one job for another or retire for good are working right up to the end. When they are not caught up in a flurry of goodbye parties or luncheons, they are training their successor, tying up loose ends, and jamming their personal effects into boxes. They routinely bring home much too much. If you are in this situation, we suggest you give yourself time to settle into your new routine before you delve into the physical evidence of a lifetime of work. Then get started!

- *Don't deny the sentiment. Whether or not you always loved what you were doing, it was a large part of your life. Revisiting your past will evoke memories, some of them funny, some of them rueful, but allow yourself to feel whatever comes up.*

- *Save a few meaningful papers or other items and discard the rest. What you save may include a certificate or award that pleased you; notes written to you by students that you find touching or funny or meaningful; an enthusiastic evaluation of your work; photographs or newspaper accounts of an important event. You may not want to save the black "Over the Hill" coffee mug your coworkers presented to you on your fiftieth birthday.*

- *Recycle whatever material or tools you can by giving them to a younger colleague or a professional library. While texts and manuals can become outdated quickly, other things do not. If your work involved physical materials, construction tools or building materials that are still on your property, you can donate them or have a sale and notify other people in the same business.*

days and saved only two sketches, which he framed. It often helps to look at the work as if it belonged to someone else, and make selections objectively.

• Take photos of the work that is left, or hire a professional who specializes in photographing works of art. You will be surprised at the way having the photograph is almost as good as the real thing. When Judi was in her twenties and was painting, she photographed all her work, especially the pieces she sold or gave away. She is happy to look at the pictures now—happier than if she had to store the actual canvases.

• *Extract the essence of your work and what it meant to you. Have a friend or family member make a videotape of you talking about the highlights of your career. Most people at first roll their eyes at the idea. But the more they think about it and how they can use various props they still have, the more it makes sense. Not only does it clarify a large part of their lives in their mind and provide some closure, their descendants will be interested.*

• *Imagine family members having to go through the cartons and files when you're gone. If you have no desire to reread outdated directives or copies of routine letters you wrote, they will have even less interest but will have to sort through them anyway.*

• *Use it or lose it. Perhaps you are holding onto copies of files (other than those that doctors, therapists, and other professionals have to keep for a certain number of years) such as notes and planners, in case you decide to write a book. It is after all not unheard of to write memoirs about everything from acting to firefighting to social work. But the time to do it is now, while the memories are still fresh. If you have a vague idea that you must write a book "someday," be aware that someday rarely comes.*

• *If you are dreading the thought of going through your work materials, do it in stages. Promise yourself that you will only discard impersonal directives and outdated bulletins, leaving your personal things intact. Or work on just one box at a time, trying to condense what is in it so you can fit two cartons into one. As with memorabilia, you may need to go through the materials several times.*

- If you're interested in selling your work, enter it in art exhibits and fairs at affordable prices. At a recent art fair on Long Island, a man who had worked for years in stained glass but was now changing his focus rented a booth and set up an attractive display. His work was beautiful and very reasonably priced and disappeared fast. By the end of 2 days, he had cleared out most of his older inventory and made enough money to begin his new endeavor. It felt more satisfying to him than simply storing the pieces in his workshop.

- Don't assume that your children and other younger relatives aren't interested in having some of your art or handcrafts. Their tastes have matured, and there may be work to which they have always felt attracted. Ask them, and give them what they would like to have. Once family members have had a chance to select what they like, broaden the invitation to friends. It can be exciting to see people's enthusiasm and your art on their walls.

  You may be interested in doing what artist Felicitas Wetter is planning. After more than 40 years of teaching, creating, and exhibiting art, she is planning to go through her vast oeuvre of prints, paintings, and assemblages and put it out on display, then invite her friends and colleagues over to select pieces they would like to have. "I don't have anyone to leave it to," she points out. "I'd rather have it go to people who would enjoy it."

- Depending on the kind of work you do, restaurants, senior centers, schools, and community organizations may appreciate having it. They are often looking to decorate spaces attractively but are usually on small budgets.

- Remember that what was most important about the work was its creation, the times you lost yourself in following your inspiration and meeting artistic challenges. Hours disappeared happily. It makes sense to save what is representative of your best creativity, work that still feels emotionally charged, and make a place to display it.

EXPIRED INTERESTS

This category might also be titled "Seemed like a good idea . . ." since these are usually specialty items, inspired by the following kind of situations:

- You wanted to be able to use a few conversational phrases on your trip to Japan, so you bought a complete set of language tapes.

- You visited an artist friend, became inspired by her decoupage projects, and stopped off at Michael's to buy the supplies to do it yourself.

- You decided to turn over a new [lettuce] leaf and bought a juicer to make all-organic juices for your family.

- You saw an exercise device for "iron abs" advertised on television and ordered one.

What is the problem with all these items? It is simply that you either never used them or tried and then abandoned the idea soon after. If you do not get in the habit of using something at the height of your enthusiasm, chances are strong that you never will. Your purchase will sit there and make you feel guilty for spending money on it.

We keep from discarding these things by telling ourselves that we will get back to them when we have more time. Or when we are "in the mood." Or the next time we go to Japan. Or when we retire. The next time you talk to someone who has retired, ask them if they have more free time now. Chances are that they will tell you that they are busier than ever before, that they don't know how they ever found the time to work.

When we were helping a couple move one time, we came across a shirt box with two blue-stamped personalized bibs and some embroidery thread. The design had been started, then abandoned. "I was making them for our twin grandsons," Frances explained. "But that kind of detail work was hard on my eyes and giving me headaches. So I stopped."

So?

"Well, I can't just throw them away!"

"How old are the boys now?"

She laughed. "Fifteen. Maybe I can find someone who would take them."

"Maybe, if they had children named Brett and Kyle."

She laughed and put the box on the discard pile.

Judi's own experience was a slight variation: Once, on vacation, she saw a trivet made of old wine corks. It was attractive, but she balked at spending $29.50 for something she "could make herself." Instead, she started saving wine corks, especially those with interesting logos. Finally she had a large plastic bagful. By then, she could not remember how the trivet had been put together or why she would want one on her table. The corks had to go.

THE GLOSSIES

National Geographic magazine was the first periodical to print artistic color photographs on glossy paper and make people realize that certain magazines should not be thrown away. Even if they never looked at a particular issue again, it would be worth something "someday." Sadly, every professional organizer has had to break the news that the magazine, unless pre-1930, has little collectible or resale value. There are just too many of them, and what was once "exotic" is now available everywhere. Some teachers might want them for geography projects, but even libraries are hesitant to take the magazines for their book sales because few people actually buy them.

The first cousins of *National Geographic* are beautiful art and photography calendars. Once the year is over, a calendar has no more objective value. But people convince themselves that they will certainly want to frame the pictures sometime or at least look at them again, so the latest edition joins the stack from previous years. Calendars that come in the mail from charities usually show appealing animals or children or scenic beauty; tossing them out unused seems a form of rejection.

Even more insidious are the calendars focusing on specific areas of interest, such as 1940s movies, a particular breed of dog, or great golf holes of the world. People often end up being given three or four of these at one holiday. The same person who likes the Impressionists may also be a fan of chocolate, cocker spaniels, and Paris.

If this is a weakness for you, remind yourself that calendars were created to be time limited. If you have to, razor out and save one or two images that you can't part with. Or ask a teacher if she could use a calendar to create classroom bulletin boards or display cases, particularly if the images follow the seasons.

HOSTESS GIFTS

If everyone who came to visit you brought you a bouquet of fresh flowers or a bottle of wine or plate of brownies, this area would not be a clutter problem. But you are just as likely to be given exquisitely wrapped jars of condiments that you can't imagine eating, exotic liqueurs, "cut-glass" vases, scented candles, or whatever else is popular and for which you don't have a use. Because these gifts show appreciation for your hospitality, they tend to hang around. It seems ungrateful to toss or give them away.

Hold that thought. In the next section, we will offer some alternatives for this category of items.

HANDMADE GIFTS

Fewer items create greater guilt than lovingly crafted gifts you can't stand. You cannot imagine why Aunt Winnie would crochet you a brown-orange-yellow afghan and expect to see it displayed across the top of your black leather sofa. And it's not only Aunt Winnie. Your best friend was into macramé years ago, and you know she would be hurt if you discarded the plant hanger she made for you— even though you haven't actually used it in years. Although you are touched by the lumpy clay ashtrays and decorated flower pots that your children or grandchildren make you, secretly you wonder how long you have to display them.

Although Aunt Winnie's color schemes may not be yours, it is important to acknowledge that in order for your tastes to be right, hers do not have to be wrong. For years, Judi and her husband, Tom, had an "Unwanted Gift Party" every January in which 30 or 40 friends would wrap up the holiday present they least liked and bring it. These could be other items as well, such as the aforementioned hostess gifts or even new things people had bought themselves that fell into the "What was I thinking?" category.

The gifts were numbered as they came through the door, and later on, numbers were passed out to the guests. At the end of the evening, the packages were opened in order of the numbering, usually amid hysterical laughter. And yet, it was surprising how often people were happy to get the Chia Head (which sprouted grass for hair), the candle in the shape of an Eskimo, the wheel of odd cheeses, the coffee mugs hand-decorated with kittens. Taste is a strange and wonderful thing.

The party also illustrated that once you are given a gift, it is yours to do with what you like. Unless you have an agreed-on stipulation (for example, "If you ever decide you don't want this painting anymore, please give it back to me"), once a gift has left the donor's hands, he does not have the right to tell you how to use it. You may want to display the afghan for a while when Aunt Winnie comes over; if you can use it in your den or at the foot of your bed, fine. If not, you can, with a clear conscience, donate it to a homeless shelter or senior citizen day care center, where it will be used often and probably treasured.

CREATE A RECORD

It is a good idea to take a photograph of Aunt Winnie with the afghan when she presents it to you and to give her a copy of the picture. The physical proof of what someone has done seems to soften the blow when it disappears from view.

As it inevitably will. Even the best handmade gifts have a shelf life. If you feel that someone else can enjoy it, pass it on. In certain cases, you can offer it back to the creator if it is part of a body of work. But do this carefully.

The important thing is to separate the gift from your relationship with the giver. You can love someone and still have different tastes. While you appreciate the time and thought he took to make or shop for a gift for you, it is a physical object, not an extension of himself that needs to be loved and cared for. If you are the giver, recognize that while you are hoping your gift is appreciated, the matter is out of your hands. You don't have the right to demand, "Where's that needlepoint pillow I gave you last Christmas?"

Realize, too, that loving thoughtfulness does not go into every gift. How many times have you heard people complain, "I've got to get them something," in a voice that indicates it is just one more obligation? Or if someone takes up pottery or woodworking or china painting, the gifts that start appearing may have more to do with a studio of surplus work rather than an item made specifically for you.

EXAMINE THE MOTIVE

Gifts, like the Trojan horse, can often come with mixed motives.

Jean, a busy New England book designer, received three mystery packages from her mother one Christmas: They were filled with old curtains, knickknacks, faded sheets, and mismatched china. There was also a note, "Here is your heritage! Don't give these things away or sell them at a yard sale!"

As Jean commented, "As if anyone would *buy* them."

She finally salvaged a cracked sugar and creamer that had been her grandmother's and a ribbon pillow from her childhood home, then tossed the rest. It was obvious Jean's mother's motive had not been to enhance her daughter's home or bequeath family treasures to her grandchildren.

FINDING NEW HOMES

We have already mentioned the Unwanted Gift Party, but there is a similar alternative for items that are not "useful" enough to donate to a charity and do not have much financial value, but which you don't want to throw away. A number of years ago, when Judi was first paring down, she and Tom had a Giveaway Brunch. They invited a number of friends over one Sunday and, after eating, opened the door to the garage. People were invited to go in and select anything they wanted from piles of china, books, records, stuffed pillows, knickknacks, sporting equipment, and handmade gifts of all sorts.

It worked out beautifully. Everyone got at least one thing they really wanted and took a few others for good measure. Judi and Tom were glad to see the items go to good homes. And the house felt 20 pounds lighter.

THE PHOTOGRAPHIC MORASS

When we ask people in workshops what is the one thing (besides family members and pets) that they would save from their homes in case of fire, the answer is overwhelmingly, "Photographs!" Then we ask them where their photographs are. They laugh sheepishly and admit they are in cartons, drawers, or the processing envelopes from the drugstore. It's actually worse if the photos have been imprisoned in albums popular in the 1970s—the kind with the self-stick adhesive pages whose strips turn brown and deteriorate the paper faster. Ironically, the earlier, black-paged albums with the adhesive corners did less harm.

Take a moment and think about where your pictures are. As long as people are not moving or scaling down, it doesn't seem a problem to have photographs in desk drawers, in closets, and in cartons, even though they know it's not the ideal solution. Since the photos can be hidden away, it does not seem a priority to organize them. But at a certain point, it has to be done.

When people protest that they "don't have time" to work on their photos, what they are actually feeling is dread at the thought of having to make so many decisions: what to frame, what to toss, what to give away, which ones are deserving of a permanent home. The pleasure of looking through the photos may also be accompanied by a fear of being sabotaged by nostalgia. There may even be the temptation to leave the sorting for the next generation. Resist! There are important reasons to do it yourself.

The best technique is to gather all your pictures in one place—processing envelopes, albums, boxes, and loose piles from drawers. Don't forget those in studio portrait folders or in frames that you no longer display. By bringing them together, you are able to see exactly what you have.

This technique is similar to what we suggest you do with papers, but more fun. It can also be a step in itself. Once you have all the photos together, you do not have to start sorting them right that moment.

WHO WAS THAT MASKED STRANGER?

Begin by sorting the photographs into rough piles, such as "Original Family," "Holidays," "Vacations," and so on. If you are at a loss for categories, see the list on page 45. As you sort, discard those photographs that are blurry or uninspired or duplicates, those of people you don't know or places you don't recognize. Yes, you can throw photographs away—not the charming studio portraits that are a hundred years old, but the curling-edged snapshots of people you can't identify, boring locales, subjects that are blurry or hard to make out. You may be tempted to save them "just in case." Just in case of what? We don't know any convincing answer to that.

While we are on the subject of throwing pictures away, don't feel that you have to save unflattering photos of people you do know. If you have a shot that makes you or someone else look like a sideshow attraction, pretend it never happened. We sometimes feel that we are duty bound to leave behind an "accurate" record. But why? Unless it was taken at a crime scene, a snapshot is not evidence. It's well and good to feel "I am who I am," but if an unexpected view of your backside makes you wince, throw it away. After all, one of the pleasures of using a digital camera is being able to immediately delete an image you don't like before it ever reaches the paper stage.

We talk more about the compulsion toward "accuracy" and the Truth Police in the next chapter, "Collaring the Paper Tiger."

THE NEXT STEP

Now that you are surrounded by piles of photographs in categories, what do you do next? Once you know the type and quantity of your photographs, it is important to identify as many as possible. Buy some archival (nonacid) labels at a craft shop or office supply store. Then, starting with the oldest photographs, which are usually ancestral, write the names and approximate year they were taken on the label. It may also help to identify them with a phrase, such as "Lou's great-aunt." Of course, *you* know who they are. You are doing this for your children, grandchildren, and other descendants. You are ensuring that people will be properly remembered. Most of us have some wonderful old photographs that we have inherited and don't have a clue who the people in them are. Afraid to discard a possible ancestor, we pass them down to other people who will have even less idea of who they are looking at.

The exceptions to labeling are vacation photographs. If you have a group of photos identified as "Italy, 1977" in an album or photo box section, they will be self-explanatory. For your own pleasure, you may want to jot down the name of the cathedral or market town or mountain you are looking at, while you can still remember it.

A side benefit of labeling photographs is that it helps you to refine your collection. If it seems too much trouble to identify a distant coworker whose last name you can't remember anyway or several far-off shots of a graduation stage, put them in the discard pile without guilt. A word about taking the time to give photographs to the people in them. It is a nice idea with vintage photos, if you know where to reach the person and will actually follow through in mailing it. As far as more recent photos of people with whom you have lost touch, assume that they have plenty of pictures of themselves.

TAMING WILD PHOTOGRAPHS

Once you have sorted, labeled, and physically scaled down your photographs, it is time to decide what to do with them. The older pictures that are irreplaceable should be kept in a fireproof safe or safe deposit box. Through the wonders of technology, however, reprints can be made and displayed, and those photographs that are creased and worn can be restored. You can have this done professionally or do it yourself if you have a good scanner and a basic program such as Adobe Photoshop LE.

Other photos or copies you may want to put in your Life Book as explained in the chapter, "This Is Your Life!" Some pictures can be framed separately or using collage mats. These mats, available at art supply stores such as Michael's, hold between 2 and 16 photos and have become more sophisticated over the years. You may also want to arrange pictures in albums, which are especially appropriate for vacations or specific events. One of the most satisfying ways to display photos is by "scrapbooking" them, using the new wonderful archival background papers. Magazines such as *Legacy* and *Somerset Studio* have creative ideas on how to incorporate photographs into art.

There are several ways to store photographs. A clear plastic sweater box makes a good receptacle for the larger, old-fashioned studio portraits, some of which may still be in frames. It can also hold children's class and team photos. For 4 by 6-inch pictures and smaller, buy several of the photo boxes with card dividers and write the category of the pictures on the tabs.

Even if you don't do anything but sort and refine your collection, you will be surprised at the peaceful feeling that comes from knowing where all your

---

PHOTOGRAPH CATEGORIES

If you are having trouble sorting photos into piles, here are some of the most popular categories:

Birthday celebrations	Original family, spouse's
Christmas/Hanukkah	Original family, yours
Class reunions	Pets
Coworkers and job sites	Proms and school activities
Extended family milestones	Retirement parties
Friends	School photographs
Graduations	Sports events
Grandchildren	Vacations
Growing up	Weddings
Homes lived in	

---

photographs are and that they are identified. When you move, you will have the satisfaction of bringing along several compact boxes or albums instead of worrying about losing pictures tossed helter-skelter in cartons and drawers.

WHY SAY GOODBYE?

The type of items we have been identifying in this chapter are things that can be difficult to part with, both because of their emotional tug and because they have little donation or resale value. Old *National Geographic* magazines, outdated work manuals, a hand-crocheted tissue box cover, Turkish language tapes, snapshots of unknown people, a 1995 Garfield the Cat calendar—why, you may be wondering, should I discard such innocuous things?

The answer lies in your mission statement. If you are trying to streamline your life, gain control of your environment, move to a smaller space, optimize where you live now, clear out your parents' home, create a spacious office or studio, make things easier for the next generation, or have that vacation house feeling by keeping only what you love and need, then everything that does not contribute to your goal has to go. You will be losing your clutter and gaining a life.

COLLARING THE PAPER TIGER

Langley Collyer and his brother Homer did not believe in scaling down. Langley, a former concert pianist, kept 14 grand pianos in their brownstone because his brother liked to hear him play. He also kept several tons of newspapers because Homer, who had been blinded and paralyzed by a stroke, would want to catch up on his reading when he regained his sight. The brothers died when Langley accidentally triggered one of the hundreds of booby traps he had set as a precaution against a changing world. A suitcase, three breadboxes, and bundles of newspapers fell on his head. Without his brother to care for him, Homer died several days later.

While few people today die of paper attacks, one man was recently trapped for 2 days under a stack of newspapers and books that collapsed on him, causing multiple injuries. Too much pulp in one place is never a good thing. You can slip on a shiny calendar lying on the floor or the stairs. Dried-out bundles of newspaper are a fire hazard. But the greatest danger may be the stress involved in trying to find an address or magazine article or sales receipt that you know you put "somewhere" for safekeeping. In vain, you approach one paper nest after another, sifting through each stack as your frustration rises. You may not even find what you are looking for until a week later when you come across it while you are searching for something else.

Added to your frustration is the stress of not knowing for certain which papers you have to save and which you can safely let go.

DECODING OUR PAPER ATTACHMENT

In our workshops, the number one complaint that participants have is that they are overwhelmed by paper. Sometimes we will mention the option of going "cold turkey"—gathering up and discarding every newspaper, magazine, catalog, supermarket flyer, and nonessential piece of paper in their homes and starting fresh the next day—just to show them their reaction. Most often the reaction is disbelieving laughter. One older man raised his hand and announced, "I'm having heart palpitations!"

Why is our relationship with paper and information so complicated? For one thing, most of us have too much respect for the printed word. Our belief in the infallibility of documents is probably rooted in elementary school when we were led to believe that everything we read in textbooks was true. Since the books had to be turned in at the end of the school year, we were not allowed to write in them or deface them in any way. We assumed that if a fact was important enough to be put in print and saved for next year's class, it had to be valuable.

The Case of the Missing Information

Given our respect for the printed word and our belief in its veracity, our fear of missing crucial information seems inevitable. We are afraid that if we discard magazines and newspapers that we haven't read, we will miss the one thing we need to know to guarantee ourselves satisfying relationships, healthy bodies, and a brimming bank account. Worse case scenario: There will be a paragraph on page 43 on "The Secret of Living Forever," and we will miss it.

Not to fear: We live in an age of information. Significant and nonsignificant findings alike are repeated ad nauseum in every newspaper, magazine, television and radio broadcast, and, of course, over the Internet. The ability to live forever would be dissected, debated, expanded on, and taken in 20 different directions.

Even if you totally ignored the media, your family, coworkers, and neighbors would be certain to let you know.

Once you heard, all you would need to do is go to "Google" on the Internet, and type in the keywords "live forever." Up would come myriad lists of articles and new Web sites devoted to that very subject. Google is so comprehensive that you could type in almost any keyword, and the information offered to you would be more varied, up-to-date and detailed than anything in your stack of unread magazines.

Taking It Personally

Another factor that complicates our relationship with paper is our tendency to take things too personally. When we receive a political flyer, community announcement, environmental handout, or hand-addressed charity appeal, we imagine that someone has worked hard to prepare this information for us; it seems disrespectful to toss it out without even looking it over. Get over it. Despite what they might like you to believe, the senders don't know anything about you except your general demographics and sometimes not even those. Since your time is limited and you have more compelling things to read, this bit of clutter will only hang around, getting in the way. You need to remind yourself, "I didn't ask for this, I don't have to know about it, and no one will know if I throw it away."

Some charities will affix a nickel or a dime to their appeal, making sure it shows through the acetate window. Not wanting to throw money away, you put it in your pile of mail to keep. But after you remove the coin, it seems churlish to discard their information. So you let the appeal lie around as clutter for a month or two and finally send a small check to the charity or throw it out feeling guilty. Either way, you end up annoyed that you have been manipulated. Next time just take the money, toss the evidence, and contribute to whomever you want.

"But It's So Attractive"

A third complicating factor is the number of magazines, catalogs, and charity calendars filled with color photographs and printed on heavy, glossy paper. Even when we know we have no rational reason to keep them, our respect for the quality makes us hesitate to just stuff them in the recycling bag— that and the soulful expression of the puppies on the front of the Animal League calendar. What you need to ask yourself is "Do I have a place for this? Will I ever look at this nature magazine again?"

Perhaps the reason that old *National Geographic* magazines are ubiquitous and worth so little as collectibles today is that as a nation, we were unable to let them go. Their early Kodachrome pictures were many people's introduction to color photography, and the techniques improved more each year. Now we have digital cameras and all types of paper to print photographs on—but some of the vestiges linger.

"Try to Remember . . ."

A final complication in the paper wars is that we don't trust our memories. We don't quite trust ourselves to remember how to program the VCR or change the vacuum cleaner filter, who sent us cards when we were in the hospital, what we wrote about *Moby Dick* in our American Literature class, or which Broadway plays we've enjoyed in the past 10 years. As far as keeping directions is concerned, most small appliances—toasters, hairdryers, electric shavers—either work or they don't, and you don't need direction booklets. The exception is manuals for more complicated machines such as computers, vacuums, and DVD players, which have troubleshooting sections you will need to refer to in case of malfunction.

As far as items such as playbills and greeting cards, these feed into the odd pressure we feel to retain a factual record of our lives. How many times has someone asked you what your favorite movies are or if you've read any good books lately, and you've come up blank? You may view it as your failure and wonder if you should be keeping lists. But another way of looking at it is that you've incorporated the experiences into your life and moved on. When something triggers your memory, you'll talk about it then. If you are living each day fully and in the moment, you don't have much time to dwell on the past.

Consolidate and Conquer

In our workshops, we sometimes advise people with a paper problem to go from room to room and collect every single piece—used envelopes, supermarket flyers, newspapers, magazines, catalogs, junk mail—and place them in a large pile. Next, bring out those papers stashed in shopping bags or stuffed randomly in desk drawers and cartons, and add them to the pile. While everyone is waiting for the magic answer, we add, "Then burn them."

Yes, it's a joke. Everyone knows you can't light a fire in the middle of your house. And, unfortunately, you can't get rid of papers that easily either.

But we do advise people to consolidate all the little nests and counter coverings in one place. This is a good technique whether you're moving or not, for two reasons: It makes everywhere else in the house or apartment look instantly tidier, and it keeps the papers in one place, so you can go back and sort through them whenever you have a chance. The pile may be a small one and make you realize that the situation is not as bad as you thought—or it may be as large as an Indian burial mound. In the second case, your reaction will probably be shock, then a tendency to laugh, then a sense of hopelessness.

Whatever your feelings about your paper pile, don't despair! Just get yourself a cup of tea (or something stronger) and start in. Rather than just reach in and assess each piece, go through quickly and pull out every flyer, supermarket handout, or newspaper, and put them in a brown grocery bag for recycling. Don't worry if you haven't read them yet; more are coming tomorrow. Next, pull out all the catalogs and magazines, and put them in two separate stacks. Isolate any photographs into their own pile.

What the remaining pile will consist of is a mixture of five categories. In some cases, the categories will overlap. But the important thing is that you are dealing with them.

It's Only Practical

This first category includes sales receipts, pay stubs, bills, tax materials, VCR instructions, warranties, addresses, driving directions, and medical records. It is a good place to start because many of these papers need to be saved. As you pick up a handful, discard old bills that have been paid; invitations to bazaars, workshops, or other events that have passed; expired coupons; ATM receipts; and sales receipts for food, gas, restaurants, and clothing you are already wearing. *Don't stop to read anything!*

What you need to keep are current bills, rebates, appeals from charities you support, and health forms to be filled out. Put these in the drawer with your blank envelopes, address labels, and stamps. Any future events that you want to attend and directions on how to get there can go on your refrigerator door or bulletin board. Receipts have several different destinations: If they are from a large purchase such as an appliance, put them in a file folder with their warranties and directions; if they are for items you wish to return, put them with your car keys; if they support your IRS return, put them in a folder marked "Current Taxes."

Items for situations that have not been resolved yet, such as medical reimbursement claims, rebates, receipts for current gifts, wedding, shower, or Bar/Bas Mitzvah invitations for which you need to buy a present, can go in a third folder, marked "Pending."

When Judi was working for a large social work agency, the most difficult things for her to be decisive about were not the bulletins and work-related papers that came across her desk daily, but flyers about baby showers, retirement or transfer luncheons, and other social events. These had a tear-off section in which you had to indicate whether you were coming or if you wanted to contribute toward a gift. In the beginning, she would shuffle them around her desk until the party was over and a de facto decision had been made. She had to learn how to make an immediate decision based on whether she knew the person and how well, and either tear off the response form and send it back, or add it to the discard pile right away.

That nearly takes care of the Practical category. You will probably be left with a little stack of business cards or torn-off address labels from envelopes. Either write down the information in your address book or toss them. VCR and DVD directions belong next to the TV. As far as grocery coupons are concerned, Marj loves them. Judi can't be bothered. But Marj recognizes that they can be far more time-consuming than they are worth. She only saves those worth 50 cents or more and only for those staple items she buys on a regular basis. A coupon holder kept in a convenient location is essential.

What about medical material? Many people stockpile nutrition newsletters and medical journals so religiously that you might imagine their contents were divinely inspired. But health is a fluid field, changing rapidly, and these should be treated like any other magazine. If you have a pile, go through them quickly, and pull out a few articles you feel are crucial—early warning signals for specific diseases, or supplements and vitamins that have been found to be beneficial. You don't need to save the more obvious stuff such as evidence that fast food chains should be visited sparingly, exercise is important, and obesity complicates medical issues.

Wishing and Hoping

This second category includes gourmet recipes torn out of newspapers, Christmas issues of decorating magazines, upscale catalogs, beauty articles, travel brochures, and computer magazines.

How can you tell if something belongs here rather than in the Practical cate-

---

HELPFUL HINTS FOR SETTING UP FILES

We believe that no one needs more than one home filing cabinet, preferably one with two drawers. Here are some ways to set it up:

- *When labeling a new file, ask yourself what word first comes to mind, and use that. If you try to be too creative, you won't remember what a particular item is filed under.*

- *Think noun. Label a file as, "Articles, Funny" not "Funny Articles." You won't be as likely to look under "F."*

- *Use general categories, such as "Directions and Warranties" or "Health Information." If your file gets too full, you can always break it down into two or more categories. But using too many specific names for file folders will clutter your drawer and make it too hard to remember what something is under.*

- *Arrange file folders alphabetically in the drawer, and put the most recent information in the front of the folder. That makes it easier to purge files by starting at the back with the oldest (and outdated) information when your file gets too full.*

- *If you need to, keep a master list of your files at the front, so that you or a family member can see at a glance what category something might be filed under.*

gory? Because rather than having to be acted on, it has the pleasant glow of "someday." You aspire to the experience it suggests, but for lack of time, money, expertise, or the proper occasion, you are unable to do it immediately. But this is an important category to cultivate. It is forward looking and inspirational and does not need to take up a lot of room.

One way to handle this category is to have a "Hope Chest." At a home-organization or office-supply store, buy a sturdy cardboard box with a separate lid. You don't want to use a ragged-edged corrugated carton that can easily be put out with the trash by mistake. With a nicer box—no, it doesn't have to be cedar-lined—you won't be as tempted to start dumping papers into it.

When you have the box, set some time aside and go through your stacks of magazines that have projects and ideas—Christmas, woodworking, craft, deco-rating, travel, and cooking magazines—and remove the articles that still excite you—then discard the rest of the magazine. Don't even think about what *may* ex-cite you in the future or what you feel should excite you, but doesn't. This is *it*.

At a stationery or office-supply store, you can buy 8½ by 11-inch clear plastic sleeves to slip each article or brochure into; if it's worth saving, it's worth being able to find again. Rather than thumbing unsuccessfully through stacks of mag-azines, you'll be able to go right to one place and find it. Keep your unused plastic sleeves in the box as well.

The benefit of using a carton rather than a desk drawer or filing cabinet is threefold. You'll be able to sit comfortably and go through the box wherever you want. You can easily clip and add items rather than hoarding magazines. Finally, since studies have shown that 90 percent of what is put into a file cabinet is never looked at again, you'll be saving information from oblivion.

The key is to have only one carton for your Hope Chest, one place to look. When you find the carton getting full, go through it again, and discard ideas that feel outdated or no longer move you. A magazine holder you once planned to build now looks amateurish; cookie recipes with pounds of sugar and butter make you cringe. If your brochures on African game parks are 10 years old, but you still hope to visit one, stop in at a travel agency, or go to the Internet, and get yourself more current information. Then discard the outdated material.

When you are tempted to add to your Hope Chest, give some thought about whether you'll actually *do* the project or a similar one that it might inspire. A friend of ours, waiting in the supermarket line, was attracted by the cover of Martha Stewart *Living*. The photograph showed hundreds of small lights shining out of a display of pumpkins. Gorgeous! She picked the magazine up, looked at the instructions, and was adding it to her cart when she came to her senses. "I suddenly thought, 'Wait a minute. You're going to clean the pulp out of six pumpkins, make several hundred holes in them with an electric drill, and rig up lights, when you can't even clean your refrigerator? I don't think so!'"

Getting Sentimental over You

The next things to look for in your diminishing pile of papers are the sentimental—old birthday cards, children's artwork, college term papers, favorable job

---

FILE LABEL IDEAS

Here are some common file categories to help you store and locate your paperwork more easily.

Appliances—directions and warranties

Articles, funny

Articles, inspirational etc.

Birthday gift ideas

Cars—repair receipts and warranties (except for battery and tire, which should go in your glove compartment)

Cartoons

Computer information

Diet and weight loss plans

Directions to friends' homes

Entertaining ideas

Family history and genealogical information

Financial information (Deferred Compensation, Social Security)

Frequent flyer conditions and information

evaluations, cute kitten pictures. Unlike Hope Chest items that are ideas for future projects, these items are passports to the past. Put greeting cards and letters in one pile, cute animal pictures and jokes from other people in another. The third is for event memorabilia such as playbills, school concert programs, and miniature drink parasols. Finally, make a pile of those items that represent your personal history such as foreign hotel receipts, old term papers, and personal journals. You may need another place for drawings and papers from your children or grandchildren. Don't obsess about what goes where; these interim piles are less important than how you will be handling them.

You'll probably feel the temptation to just toss everything in your Memorabilia Box (see Chapter 12) and move on to something else. But resist. *That* box has to hold everything of emotional importance from your life.

Glasses/contact lens prescriptions and providers

Health and dental insurance forms—blank

Health and beauty ideas

Health records

Helpers—plumbers, lawn care, painters, babysitters, electricians, etc.

Home—copy of deed, home improvement receipts

Important papers (copies of birth, marriage certificates, passports, vehicle titles,
    wills, military discharge, DNRs, etc.)

Insurance—car, home, life

Investments

Menus, takeout

Pay stubs (if your income fluctuates)

Prescription information

Pet information

Receipts, holiday gifts

Receipts, other—appliance, furniture, camera, etc.

Résumés

Retirement information

Sometimes when we are doing a consultation with people on how to scale down, they say, "But I'm very sentimental," as if it is a blood type. Perhaps you feel that wallowing in the past or that being moved to tears is part of your personality. But even if it is, how much do you want to feed into it? Staying surrounded by things that remind you of past experiences or to which you respond predictably can keep you from moving ahead in your life.

Even the worst cases of sentimentality can be taught to discriminate between what truly means something to them and what is a knee-jerk response.

Here are some of the culprits that we all face.

Greeting cards

Yes, there are people who can receive a birthday, sympathy, or Christmas card, smile or feel touched, then let it go immediately. But most of us can't. We imagine how the giver went to the trouble of picking out just the right message, then mailed it or delivered it to us with a gift. The card has entered our orbit and become part of our personal history. Fortunately for most of us, unless a card has a warm personal message or makes us laugh all over again, we realize it does not need to be saved.

Yet for some people, a card stirs up the spectre of keeping an accurate personal history. It is the same demon that persuades us that we have to save unflattering photographs in the interests of "truth." Again, why? The Truth Police will not be coming to your door. If you need to remember that you received 50 get-well cards when you were in the hospital, pick out your favorite, write on the back, "Also received messages from . . ." and list the other senders before recycling those cards.

If you do not have this compulsion toward accuracy and completion, it may be hard to imagine the feelings of someone who does. But if you recognize this trait in yourself, we are giving you permission to let go of any cards in this current pile (or in your Memorabilia Box) that are not handmade, have a written message that still warms your heart, or which will make you laugh out loud 5 years from now. And we're not even saying you have to keep those.

Be even stricter with vacation postcards from friends, invitations to parties or events you enjoyed but did not find memorable, and calendar-style cards from businesses and charities. You *can* toss ugly Christmas greetings and cut up the images on the beautiful ones to use as gift tags or put them in small frames to display in December.

"But it's so cute!"

Many times, sentimental items come from other people in the form of adorable animal photos, anything to do with angels, or newspaper clippings and jokes they think you will be interested in. Part of the pile that you're going through now may also have items that you are saving to mail to other people. Marj keeps a folder and dates each paper. If it hasn't been sent in a month, it won't be. Sometimes, she sends a quick e-mail to the potential recipient describing the article. Their response (or lack of it) can determine whether or not she mails it.

Think of these papers the way you would a grapefruit half. You cut it open and enjoy the fruit, then toss out the rind. Read the story about the new mayor of your former hometown, smile at the joke or animal antics, marvel at the truth-is-stranger-than-fiction anecdote—then say goodbye. If the item isn't something practical that you can use in the future, and it isn't a future dream for your Hope Chest, you have nowhere to put it but in the recycling bag.

Evidence of things past

Most events we attend come with something to remember them by, whether programs from concerts and plays, artists' lists from exhibitions, bulletins from church services, or handouts from workshops and seminars. The best thing you can do is return home empty-handed, leaving whatever it is discreetly on a chair. That folder or piece of paper seems harmless enough. But like a salesman who gets his foot in the door and is suddenly inside your home, it will be just as hard to get rid of as he would be. Despite your best intentions, you will never look at the paper again, except for a quick, annoyed glance when it keeps resurfacing.

Vacation evidence

Leftover materials from the trips we take are chronic offenders. Besides the photographs and the postcards you buy, you also bring home matchbooks, restaurant and hotel receipts—particularly charming if they're in another language—and brochures from the places you visited. Most museums, cathedrals, historic homes, or national monuments have arranged it so that you pass through the gift shop on your way out. Thinking that you'd like to learn more about what you have just seen or recall it in the future, you buy a glossy illustrated book. But unless you read it that same day, the chances are remote that you ever will. (Ask us how we know.) The book comes home with you, hangs around in your suitcase, then finds a stack of magazines. All you can do with it is offer it to your local library for their vertical files or give it to a book sale. Storing it on your bookshelf won't *make* you read it.

Go to the next category in the stack you have collected.

Crucial Papers

A crucial paper is one that sooner or later someone else will need to see. The amount of papers that fit into this category is actually small, and they can be kept in a fire safe or safe deposit box. For most people, they include the following:

Adoption or naturalization papers
Birth and death certificates
Deeds to homes and other properties
Health proxy information
Marriage license/divorce papers
Military discharge papers
Passports
Titles to automobiles
Wills

If these are lost, they can be replaced, but not without a lot of trouble and expense. Better to know where they are and keep them safe.

Another kind of paper that someone else might demand to see is your income tax return—or, rather, the materials supporting it. One of the most common questions people ask at our workshops is "How long do you have to keep your tax returns?" This is never a casual question. Until a few years ago, in public opinion polls, "Fear of being audited" was almost as prevalent as "Fear of dying."

Technically, the Internal Revenue Service can audit your returns for the past 2 years. In certain cases, they can go back 7 years. If they believe you have deliberately tried to defraud the government, they can audit back as far as they like.

We give people this information but also add that it is a matter of comfort level. A copy of a completed tax form and supporting materials does not take up a lot of room. If you get a sturdy cardboard box, and layer them inside by year, you can probably keep your returns forever, if that is what makes you feel secure.

Disposable Papers

Look at what is left in your pile. In a perfect world, there would be nothing. In the real world, there will probably still be a calendar from your heating company, yesterday's newspaper, an appeal from a charity that slipped past you, directions for a vanished appliance, a photo of someone else's grandchild, 20 years of *Plumbing Supplies Newsletter,* address stickers for places you no longer live. (If you think that people don't hold onto those, think again.)

Take a deep breath, and get rid of them all. You'll be so glad that you did.

PAYING THE BILLS WITHOUT PAYING THE PRICE

Keeping track of paying the bills offers an example of paperwork gone wrong. When you pay bills, you send one part back with your check and save the other portion "for your records." But why? That piece of clutter is no more proof of payment than your check stub or carbon and less proof than your canceled check, if you still receive one. If there is no past balance in next month's bill, you know your payment is in their computerized system. Monthly credit card statements can go in a drawer or envelope marked "Taxes."

You can even avoid the problem of extra pieces of paper altogether by paying your bills electronically. Most companies list their Web site on your bill, and if you are comfortable using the computer and the Internet, you can go to their site and make arrangements to have your payments either deducted from your bank account or charged to a credit card. There are also services that will pay all your bills electronically to save you from having to visit multiple Web sites to pay them all. Otherwise, you can speak to your bank directly about setting up the system. Many banks offer free overdraft protection, so if one bill is unexpectedly high, your payment or checks won't bounce but will be paid out of your $1,000 monthly reserve.

5

THE TYRANNY OF COLLECTIONS

Once upon a time, you found yourself attracted to cows. Or perhaps it was old screwdrivers. Or anything issued yearly such as ornaments, Coca-Cola trays, commemorative plates, or Hess trucks. You displayed them, and people noticed your interest; for your birthday or the holidays, you began to get more. Finally, you had an entire shelf or wall display or room and decided that enough was enough. But like the Sorcerer's Apprentice, you were unable to turn off the flow. Soon even casual acquaintances were leaving frogs or commemorative beer cans on your doorstep.

Not everyone has the collector's temperament. Marj never got into it; Judi understands the mindset all too well. There are theories that the instinct to amass things goes back to the hunter-gatherer age when our ancestors were searching for what they needed to survive. The more animal skins or red meat or berries they collected, the better off they were nutritionally and in community standing.

WHY COLLECT?

There are many reasons why people collect things. If you are a person who enjoys doing so, you may feel that *why* you do it doesn't really matter. It is part of your personality, a characteristic you enjoy, and you are not about to give up collecting anytime soon. Yet if you are trying to scale down, it helps to understand the specific prompts to which you are responding. Doing so may help you deal with your collections in a more effective way.

The Thrill of the Hunt

Snaring a prize collectible from an antique dealer, tag sale, or on eBay can be just as thrilling as bagging an elephant and a lot easier to bring home. There is the same search and then skill, negotiation, and competition. Finding something you have been searching for for years and at an affordable price is a heady experience. The downside, of course, is that once the item joins the rest of your collection, you tend to stop *seeing* it. Your focus is on the next expedition, the next prize.

The Need for Completion

In the 1930s, when Depression Glass began to be popular, manufacturers started making it in a variety of colors. Trying for as large a profit as possible in difficult times, they created many accessory pieces—probably not fully realizing the challenge they were setting for future collectors. Yet manufacturers have always known about the pull of completion and for generations have dated plates, trays, ornaments, and model cars, bringing a new one out every year. Even children like to have complete "sets."

A Purpose in Life

This is not meant in the largest sense, as in family or philanthropy or art, but as a way to spice up your everyday life. It is fun to have a goal beyond mindless routines or browsing in shops, something that adds zest to your activities, especially when traveling. For some people, purpose lies in taking the perfect photograph; for others, it means seeking out a particular kind of silver or hard-to-find book. A book dealer told us the story of a tourist who came into his shop and asked about an out-of-print volume. After a moment, the bookseller realized, delighted, that he actually had the book for sale. But when he told the man, his face fell. "I guess I'll have to *buy* it then."

Since his search was ended, he would have to find a new purpose.

As a Way to Be Sociable

Half the fun of collecting is being able to share your experiences with other like-minded people. There are many ways for collectors to meet each other—at sales and auctions, through newsletters, periodicals, and Web sites. Often, there are conventions or swap meets. Even though these people are your competitors, who better understands your feelings and the true value of your trophies of the hunt?

If you've ever gone to an estate or tag sale early in the morning, you can watch the dealers and collectors opening their trunks or van doors to show the others treasures they've recently bought. Get close enough, and you will hear them happily trading war stories.

As an Investment

In our workshops, people frequently ask about saving particular items because they "may be worth something someday." And some of them will. Old tin toys have kept their value and increased as they have become rarer. So have genuine Picassos, books signed by John Steinbeck, early Steuben Glass pieces, rare stamps, and Beatles memorabilia. But as we discuss later in this chapter, most of what people hold onto is "stuff," which will only marginally increase in value, if at all, and not be worth the room it is taking up. To be really collectible, items should be in their original boxes—and you can imagine how much space they use that way.

As a Carryover from Childhood

In the past, parents encouraged children to have a hobby that would keep them quietly occupied. Sometimes, it was model airplane making or crocheting. Other times, it was saving matchbooks or postcards or stamps and putting them into albums. Boys collected coins and model cars; girls had shelves of horse figurines and Storybook Dolls. Not only are some of these collections hard to get rid of now for sentimental reasons, they introduced us to a new way of experiencing the world and set up patterns that may still be with us.

To Fulfill an Emotional Need

When her children were grown, Judi's mother discovered antique dolls. It could have been triggered by an empty nest, but Judi thinks it went deeper than that. Her mother was the daughter of a Methodist minister, moving from church to church in the Western frontier. "My mother always talked about how her doll would disappear a few days before Christmas, then show up under the tree in new clothes. There was very little money to buy gifts, and my mother was thrilled. And yet—by collecting bisque dolls to the point where she eventually had to have a separate doll room, I think she was either trying to replicate a happy experience or was finally getting the new dolls she had secretly yearned for."

Items may also fill a void that is normally satisfied by other things. During one of our workshops, a woman who collected antique linens and Precious Moments figurines raised her hand. "My husband wants me to cut down on my collections, but I love all of them! They're like my children." She went on to explain that she had nine sets of china she loved as well as a menagerie of glass animals. Although we talked about ways in which she could scale down, we could not ask the larger questions in a group setting about what was missing from her life.

As an Unconscious Habit

In her wonderful book, *Clear Your Clutter with Feng Shui,* Karen Kingston tells the story of a woman whose home she visited as part of her practice. There were ducks everywhere—on sheets, placemats, and knickknack shelves—Karen counted more than 100 in all. But when she asked the woman, "What's with the ducks?" her client blinked at her. "What ducks?" she asked. She had gotten so used to buying anything with a duck on it that it no longer registered consciously.

An extreme case perhaps. But you may have gotten into the Pavlovian habit of picking up something with a particular motif whether you need it or not.

THE TOP 5 COLLECTING DILEMMAS

Whatever your reasons for collecting, when you are looking to scale down or live in a smaller space, situations that you've learned to live with suddenly seem problematic. These are some of the most common:

1. You've outgrown your collection and want to move on, but you can't stem the tide that keeps rolling in.

At the beginning of the chapter, we talked about how the initial thrill of collecting sports memorabilia or Lladro statues or leather-bound books could wane. You reach the place where you either don't want any more, or you have grown more knowledgeable and are only interested in a certain kind. "Certain kinds" are usually more expensive and harder to find.

Even if you are able to tell one or two people exactly what you want and have them understand, most of the other people in your life will need to be discouraged from buying you *any*. The best time to let people know, of course, is not after you've just opened your latest faux Hummel. Choose an occasion far away from your birthday or the holidays and tell people, "You know, I really used to love getting _____. But I think I've had my fill, and with having to scale down, I don't have room for any more. I've already had to let some of them go."

Most people, when hearing that you are actually downsizing your collection, will get the message. You may have to repeat it more than once for those people who tell you, "I know you said you didn't collect _____ anymore, but this one was so cute I just couldn't resist!"

You can agree that it's cute, and thank them graciously; then dispose of it after a week or two.

2. You're ready to relinquish a collection that you no longer love, but don't know what to do with it.

In order to know in which direction you want to go, you need to first decide if your collection has any monetary value. Certain collectibles appreciate in value, particularly if they are no longer being made or are made of sterling silver or other precious metals. Condition also makes a difference; if an item is rusted, chipped, or stained, it probably won't appeal to other collectors. To find out if your collection is worth selling, you can research it on eBay by seeing what comparable pieces are selling for. This process is covered in "Finding Good Homes," which also explains how to profitably liquidate a collection.

There is no reason why you cannot give part of your collection as gifts to people you know would enjoy them. Judi's mother refined her antique doll collection by giving dolls to various family members at Christmas; everyone was happy to get one of these beauties, and her granddaughters were especially thrilled. Judi's mother-in-law gave her two beautiful Art Nouveau pieces that Judi had admired at her house for years. They were appreciated long after other birthday gifts could not be remembered.

The other kind of collection has more sentimental than monetary value. It includes things such as animal memorabilia (stuffed toys, figurines, prints, and knickknacks), artwork by unknown artists, and sets of classics that aren't first editions—just old. Certain things such as china or vintage cameras have value, but are often difficult to sell. Your most satisfying course is to recognize the pleasure this collection has given you and either look for a younger collector who would appreciate having it or find the right thrift shop.

There is no need to go cold turkey with your collection; if you want, keep one or two favorites that are symbolic of what you once loved.

3. You're still emotionally interested in a particular category, but your collection has gotten much too large.

Even if you don't collect vintage pinball machines like one friend of ours, all collections have a way of outgrowing their space. When that happens, it is time to refine it. If you spend much time with other collectors, you are probably familiar with the process. If not, one way to begin is with triage. Take three pieces from your collection, decide which one you like the least, and set it aside. Go on to the next three items, and do the same thing. And so on, until you've gone through everything. What you are doing is downsizing by discarding the group you like least and keeping the two-thirds closest to your heart. Can you cheat a little? Of course. As we mentioned in the chapter on specific techniques, when you make up your group, there's no harm in making sure that a nonfavorite is included. You'll still end up with the same number of pieces to let go at the end.

If your collection has a monetary value, an alternative is to trade in several of the pieces you don't want for something more valuable that you do—either a straight swap with another collector, or by selling the unwanted pieces, then buying the better one. You'll still have lessened the size of your collection and have something that makes you even happier.

4. You've been saving things you feel *might* be valuable someday, but you have too many and don't know which ones are worth saving.

As mentioned, we are asked about this very frequently in our workshops by people who are stashing away current baseball cards, McDonald's toys, Precious Moments figurines, and newspaper headlines from important events. We try to explain why the original collectibles such as early Pez candy containers, a Jackie Robinson baseball card, or newspapers detailing the sinking of the *Titanic* have value now—few people thought to save them, and they became scarce. But once a category is designated as "collectible," millions of people begin saving it, and the monetary value plummets.

If you are still determined to hold onto "potentially" valuable items, at least do it in an organized way, and research what you have. You will quickly learn what is valuable and what is too common. But why hold onto items you do not love just because you think they might be valuable in 40 or 50 years? You may not even be around to see it; meanwhile, it is just more stuff to store and look after.

And in the end it might backfire. Ken, a Chicago lawyer, had a lot of older Christmas and commemoratives stamps his father had saved. When he decided to seek his fortune and took them to a reputable dealer, he was shocked to hear that not only were they not as valuable as he had fantasized, they were worth less than their original price. "Use them on letters," the dealer advised him kindly. "They're still worth face value."

5. Collecting is part of your personality—a part you enjoy—and won't just disappear.

If you've read this far into the chapter, chances are that you are one of the people for whom collecting adds zest to life. We are not suggesting that you give it up, only suggesting that there are other ways to experience it.

THE BETTER COLLECTOR

Scaling down a collection begins with scaling down the way you think about what you possess. Here's how you can do it and still keep the joy that you get from the process.

Make Sure You're Still in Love

A true-life situation: Joan, a colleague of Judi's, began collecting antique valentines right out of college. She loved the beautiful German pop-ups, the movables, the clever postcards, the penny dreadfuls. People began giving them to her as gifts. In the 1960s and 1970s, it was possible to buy valentines and postcards cheaply. Then early valentines were "discovered" and became expensive. Joan lost interest in actively collecting them. But she knew that they were in the closet, organized in albums, and that if she wanted to, she could look at them—though she never did. Finally, after several years, she decided to offer a few of them on eBay and was astonished at the amount of money she received. No longer in love with her collection, she liquidated it, saving only a few favorites, and used the proceeds to travel.

This is an area where it is important to be honest with yourself. If your entire collection were to disappear, would you be devastated or only mildly regretful? If someone showed up on your doorstep and offered you good money for your collection, would you slam the door in her face or start looking for packing materials? Maybe rather than trying to find room for it in your new space, the time has come to say goodbye.

Choose a Representative

Many collections did not begin as collections at all but started accidentally with one or two things, then took on a life of their own. Our friend Vicki found that this had happened with her son's stuffed animals, which were left behind when he was grown. "Since it was a group of items that all had the same meaning behind them, I kept just one or two. Instead of keeping *all* of Glen's stuffed animals from his youth, I kept the one that had the strongest memory attached to it, which was his Fievel Mousekawitz."

Think about Collecting Intangibles

When Judi was traveling in Russia on a river cruise, she heard people talking about the Travel Century Club. This is an organization for people who have traveled to 100 or more countries out of the 317 that they recognize and list. They have meetings and luncheons and compare experiences and notes. A look at their Web site, www.travelerscenturyclub.org, may inspire you to reach for your passport.

This is collecting on a large scale, which involves keeping a record but not physical objects—in much the same way that birdwatchers create a "life list" of species they hope to see. They check them off on the list when they find one but don't bring home the birds themselves. Other travelers collect wild animals by photographing them; people "save" ornate manhole covers, Art Deco architecture, grave monuments, and laundry lines by taking pictures. It's true that you have the physical photos, but putting the best of them in an album with brief notes takes up far less room.

Collect Smaller

When we were growing up, a lot of us collected baseball cards, stamps, coins, postcards, Ginny dolls, or arrowheads—none of which took up much room. In fact, we were encouraged to have a hobby that was physically manageable. Playing cards were traded at school for their back illustrations, Gainsborough's "Blue Boy," or TWA souvenirs, and even ice cream cups had cardboard lids with photos of movie stars.

This nostalgic memory is presented here to remind us that we were once happy with something smaller than a garage full of Classic cars or shelves of Lladro statuary. If you have the true collecting instinct, there are many smaller things to pique your interest. A friend of ours now collects old silver napkin rings; they take up little space, have historical charm and individuality, and can be used at special dinners. If you enjoy good wine and mark special occasions with it, remove the labels, and keep them in an album with notes about the occasion and the wine itself. You can do the same with playbills if you enjoy the theater.

Instead of buying posters or descriptive books whenever you go to a museum or historic site, pick out the one postcard you find most inspiring or beautiful, then bring it home and put it in an album or photo box. Going through the collection every now and then will continue to give you pleasure. And when an image no longer resonates, send a note on it to a friend.

Collect for Others

Charitable organizations need specific things. Local Head Start programs and Third World countries alike can use children's books, which you can pick up inexpensively and in good condition at library sales or thrift shops. Other organizations need everything from new toothbrushes and toothpaste to shoes and clothing. Searching out these items yourself can be more fun and feel less intrusive than soliciting people for financial donations.

If you have children or grandchildren in the actively collecting stage, you can be on the lookout for items they want and give them to them for holidays and birthdays. You'll still have the thrill of the hunt without having to keep your prizes yourself.

Speaking of the next generation, if you have valuable collections, make sure that you leave written notes about the items and their specific value. It's not as much of a tragedy if they fall cheaply into another collector or antique dealer's hands as it is for them to be tossed in the trash.

Finally, look at how your collections—or those of an older relative—fit in with your Scaling Down Mission Statement. The path of least resistance is to hold on to everything, but it will not take you where you want to go.

6

THE SECRET LIFE OF CLOTHING

Last year, Dorothy, a client whom Judi was helping to relocate, sold her house and moved from the East Coast into her daughter's spacious California home. The plan was for her to relax with her grandchildren and finally do as she pleased, and she was looking forward to that. Moving out West, she took only a few favorite pieces of furniture, books—and her wardrobe. Her collection of clothes, which she will not part with, measures 16 feet when hanging up. Since there is not room in her own closet, most of it is hanging on a rack in her son-in-law's basement office. "It's not as if her clothes are that good," her daughter confided to a friend. "Lots of faded skirts and blouses. And suits! All you need where we are is a couple of pairs of shorts."

There is no doubt that clothing is one of the most complicated areas of our lives. It is easy for organizers to say, "If you haven't worn it for a year—or 2 years—give it away," but that rule doesn't begin to address the relationship we have with what we wear or, in many cases, what we have and don't wear. Why does Ted, a widower of otherwise simple tastes, have a collection of several hundred short-sleeved cotton shirts in closets throughout his home, shirts that appear identical to the naked eye?

What about the persistent taboo that keeps us from not only not wearing the same clothing 2 days in a row but also not even in the same week? We'll reach for something, then think, "Oh, no, I just wore that Tuesday." When we point out to audiences that in the early 20th century, men and women wore the same suit "to business" every day, washing out the blouse or shirt when necessary, we are met with amused disbelief.

Before we discuss ways to tame your wardrobe into a more manageable collection, it is helpful to understand the emotional complexities of clothes: why it is so difficult to put together outfits we feel good wearing, and why it is so hard to let go of what we own. The presence of clothing in our lives encompasses how we feel about shopping, the persona we are hoping to create, the way we want to be identified by strangers, and feelings that lie deep in childhood. Some people treat clothes like a uniform; others get great pleasure from exploring texture, color, and pattern and combining them to create art.

Perhaps you are wondering where we weigh in on this complicated subject, since we will be doling out advice. We met at a boarding school in Florida when Judi was 15. Marj, who had graduated a few years earlier and attended college in the area, had just started teaching at the school. In Judi's memory, Marj was always

THE 10 TOP REASONS WHY WOMEN DON'T WEAR THE CLOTHES IN THEIR CLOSETS

- *"It makes me look fat."*
- *"It doesn't go with anything."*
- *"I'm still looking for the button to sew back on."*
- *"It's not quite right for work (or anything else)."*
- *"Since it was a gift, I really should wear it a few more times before giving it away."*
- *"It's ugly!"*
- *"It needs to be shortened."*
- *"It isn't my color."*
- *"The handwork is beautiful—but nobody wears muumuus anymore."*
- *"The top still fits, but the pants are a little tight."*

**THE 10 TOP REASONS WHY MEN DON'T WEAR
THE CLOTHES IN THEIR CLOSETS**

- *"It needs to be ironed."*
- *"It was a Father's Day gift."*
- *"The last time I wore it, everybody laughed."*
- *"I don't wear suits except to funerals."*
- *"There's a pair of slacks somewhere that matches the jacket. But I haven't seen them lately."*
- *"I refuse to wear a shirt with baby Cupids all over it."*
- *"It needs to be cleaned."*
- *"The collar is hell on my neck."*
- *"I think the moths have gotten to it."*
- *"My wife won't let me throw it away."*

---

gorgeously dressed. It wasn't just that the outfits she wore matched perfectly; she had started modeling as a young teenager to increase her wardrobe and wore her clothes with panache.

And Judi? Two memories from that time will suffice. In the first, her house-mother is berating her for having everything jumbled together in her dresser drawer—a gold evening purse next to a pair of woolly sweat socks, under a crumpled half-slip. In the second, when Judi comes downstairs wearing a black cotton dress (evidently slightly lint-covered), Marj comments, "That dress looks like you've been lying on your bedspread!"

Marj is still interested in clothes and is sympathetic to people with large wardrobes. Judi has become a minimalist who can happily wear anything in her closet. But both agree that they have never met anyone who literally had too few clothes, a client to whom they had to say, "Gee, you've only got two sweaters and one pair of pants. Before we do anything else, we'd better go shopping!" That includes people receiving public assistance. As long as thrift shops offer opportunities to "fill up a bag for $1.00," and charities freely distribute clothing in good condition, every American can have a large wardrobe.

This includes men, who can also have too many clothes, particularly in the area of shirts and ties. But they do not usually have as complicated a relationship with what they wear. They have fewer categories to consider and fewer style choices. So while they can use the steps on paring down, the following discussion may not apply to them.

HOW IT ALL STARTED

Our relationship with clothing began, literally, at birth. We were dressed up by our parents to be photographed, and we were told how cute we looked. We learned that there were different clothes for boys than for girls and certain outfits for "dress" and for "play." Even as toddlers, we were forming attachments to certain colors and patterns and learning that getting something new was supposed to be exciting. *Supposed* to be, because many of us were resistant to the stiffness and unfamiliarity of new clothes. We did not know how we would feel in them or what our experiences wearing them would be.

Fast forward to school. Unlike Thoreau's admonition to beware of enterprises that require new clothes, we embraced the tradition of wearing something new for the first day of school; in fact, some of us had a whole new wardrobe, since we had physically outgrown our old clothes. A number of the items were hand-me-downs from brothers and sisters, cousins, and the children of our parents' friends, and since kids' clothes were not yet trendy, we looked fine. Clothes consciousness was only beginning to dawn, though we were already being taught appropriateness: You could not wear a ruffled organdy dress to school; cowboy chaps and a six-gun holster were not suitable for Sunday school.

Once we reached junior high school age, most girls were very conscious of what they were wearing, comparing themselves to the way everyone else was dressed and the latest photos in *Seventeen* magazine. Except for a few individualists, clothes seemed all important. You might think that such a focus would have taught us how to dress and shop so that as adults we would be able to avoid overstuffed closets filled with not-quite-right items. Alas, we were too busy copying what was "in" or trailing after the latest fads, rebelling against the clothes our parents thought appropriate, and trying out different identities ourselves.

It is interesting to ask people what one item of clothing they were most attached to as teenagers, and why. Judi's was a chartreuse green nylon jacket she bought when she was 14 that had patches with clever traffic sayings such as "Beware of Dangerous Curves" and "Soft Shoulders." Wearing it made her feel highly visible and dangerous. Marj loved a felt poodle skirt with an appliquéd dog and chain leash because it was *not* a hand-me-down. When Judi polled her friends, Gail, who had to wear uniforms for parochial school, enjoyed coming home and changing into Levi's, a cardigan worn backward, and penny loafers; it made her feel like a leader instead of the follower she was at school. Another friend, Becca, loved a particular poor boy sweater and flowered skirt because she felt it would attract "blond surfer boys."

These clothes all met emotional needs for us as adolescents. Unfortunately, they did not teach us how to dress as adults.

WHAT WE LEARNED—AND DIDN'T LEARN

What did we learn from our own families that still influences us now?

- Wait until it goes on sale.

- Why should I pay full price? You'll just outgrow it.

- A special occasion calls for a new outfit.

- There's nothing wrong with hand-me-downs!

- We don't have money to waste on "fads."

- You worry too much about what you wear and not enough about your grades.

- That makes you look "cheap!"

- You can never go wrong with navy.

- Always buy good quality; people can *tell*.

- You mustn't wear white shoes before Memorial Day.

- Try to be unique; you don't want to see yourself coming and going.

- Dark colors are more slimming (and you need slimming!)

These reactions to clothing are like tics—innate, minor reflexes we aren't even aware of most of the time. One reason that these tics affect what is in our closets now and our ability to scale down is because of the push/pull of our response. Sometimes we listen to the admonition. Sometimes we rebel against it. But when we have not made peace with these voices from our past, we have a lot of physical evidence to show for it.

Worst case example: You buy an expensive, tailored navy wool suit (on sale), thinking that it will go with everything and can be worn on many different occasions. Instead, no matter what you pair it with, the outfit looks as if you are aspiring to join the Visiting Nurse Society. Still, there are so many good reasons why it *should* work that you can't give it away. It hangs respectably in your closet.

What didn't we learn? Except for the "instructions" we received growing up, many of us were never taught *how* to dress or how to buy clothes. We did not consciously consider what we wanted our clothing to convey about us. It was assumed that we would learn by doing or by watching what other people did. But consider: Fashion magazines show photographs of extremely expensive, cutting-edge outfits that you would not actually be able to wear to the places you normally go—unless you hang out on the Riviera or ride on Mardi Gras floats. Setting the magazines aside, you head for a department store and find racks and racks of one particular color combination or style, neither of which take *your* needs into consideration. So you do the best you can, and once in a while, something works.

Our feeling is that an understandable ignorance is the largest single reason that people have untamed clothes closets. They have tried hard over the years but bought the wrong things. Not drastically wrong, but wrong for them. So they have a closet full of not-quite-right clothing—not bad enough to get rid of but not good enough to wear happily. When they stand in front of the closet door and think, "I have nothing to wear," they are essentially right. There is nothing that meets the triple criteria of fitting well, making them feel attractive, and being appropriate for the occasion.

We'll address this more when we talk about scaling down and building up wardrobes, but it is helpful to look first at a few of the other reasons we ended up in clothing hell.

HOW WE ENDED UP IN CLOTHING HELL

The next time you catch yourself staring at your busting closet or trying to jam one more pair of pants into a dresser drawer, don't lose heart. It *is* possible to scale down, once you understand the cultural and emotional biases that keep us overloaded and underdressed.

Emotional Ambivalence

Even though we need to wear clothes every day, many people feel guilty about spending time focusing on them. We feel that there are other, more worthwhile pursuits. It is still virtuous in our society to claim that you never pay attention to what you wear. Although some of these feelings go back to the Puritans and our Protestant ethic, we also have the example of Roman Catholic nuns in traditional habits, Amish communities dressing "plainly," and Buddhist monks in robes, connecting piety with a lack of interest in outer adornment.

Interestingly, other, nonreligious groups feel ambivalent as well. Artists are notorious for scorning everything but overalls or paint-stained jeans, signaling that they are not going to buy into society's conventions—as well as the fact that they have *serious* work to do. The most famous photograph of Albert Einstein shows him with uncombed hair, wearing an unraveling cardigan sweater. He was excused, of course, because he was busy working on the theory of relativity.

Some of the rest of us without that excuse may also pretend that what we are wearing doesn't matter—until we need a special outfit in a hurry and buy something quickly, then find that it has joined the other not-quite-right things in our closet. We feel forced to hold onto these not-quite-right clothes because we don't know what to replace them *with*.

Clothes As Reform School

Many of us have had people close to us who tried to make us into something different by giving us particular clothing. In her book, *The Language of Clothes,* Alison Lurie captures the experience perfectly when she describes how, when she was first married, she dressed in a Radcliffe Beatnik style. "My mother-in-law, hoping to remodel me into a nice country-club matron, frequently presented me with tiny-collared, classically styled silk blouses and cashmere sweaters in white, beige, or pale green, which I never wore and could not give away because they were monogrammed." Part of the reason they were monogrammed was so that there would be no mistaking for whom they were intended.

When we are given clothing that is "not us," it is helpful to look for the message behind the gift. Husbands and wives often buy the kind of clothes that *they* would like to see their partner wear, not what they think the other person will like. Size is a grenade in a gift bag. If the item is a size or more too small, we are not sure whether to be flattered that we appear so slender or be insulted at a hint that we should lose some weight. If the item is several sizes too large, we are insulted, period.

What happens to these clothes? Sometimes we wear them and are intrigued by the new aspect of ourselves that is created. Other times we feel uncomfortable and resentful at being coerced. Siblings can take over the task from parents or grandparents. Pam, a Long Island artist originally from South Africa, was given what Pam calls a "Connecticut skirt" by a conservative cousin to wear when she goes to visit her in Westport—rather than one of her more "flamboyant" outfits. Pam, incidentally, is in her seventies.

Another example: Eleanor's sister, who dresses beautifully, consistently gives Eleanor cheap, shoddily made outfits for her birthday. Whatever the message is, it is not a positive one.

Old Habits Dying Hard

Some of us can remember back to when a "Sunday outfit" meant a purse and shoes that matched as well as a hat and gloves that complemented each other. Gradually the gloves disappeared, followed by the dressy hats, and women rebelled against uncomfortable shoes. Many began using just one bag most of the time, circumventing the problem of "I left it in my other purse!" Manufacturers responded and stopped making handbags in pastel colors, concentrating on neutrals that went with everything.

You would think, then, that when Marj or Judi help a client scale down, having too many purses would not be an issue. Think again. Handbags burst out of closets in tooled leather, denim, vinyl with designer's initials, clutch size, and tote-bag size, and whatever else you can imagine. They are no longer keyed to shoes or outfits but have been created for novelty. Because they have no designated purpose, most of them are jumbled together in a corner of the closet and forgotten. The purse habit, kept alive by manufacturers and advertisers, has outlived its purpose.

If some of the accessories in your closet *are* vintage, think about displaying them for your own pleasure. When Marj talks about "Wylla's Paris hats," it is easy to imagine a glamorous collection on a shelf, even if you have never met her sister. Interesting purses or pieces of artistic jewelry can be hung in a column on a bedroom wall. Think about the collections of baseball and golf caps that many men display hanging from pegs or lined up on a shelf. Most of them will never be worn, but it pleases their owners to look at them.

Shoe-a-holism

Judi's sister-in-law, Liz, believes that most women are shoe-a-holics. Even Liz's mother, who lives in senior housing, estimates that *she* has about 36 pairs of shoes. They have identified Judi as not one of them because she does not own a pair of red high heels. Actually, Judi has only nine pairs of shoes, including sandals, Reeboks, and black dress heels, because that is the number that her shoe rack holds.

After speaking to many clients, Judi and Marj understand better why so many women have so many shoes. Shoes complete an outfit nicely. Feet are an extension of the leg, which is considered sexy, and high heels enhance its natural curve. Shoes can be pleasurable to shop for. As Dale puts it, "You don't have to worry about feeling *fat*. Even if you have to go to the next half-size, your feet will look fine. Pants might be a horror show, but your feet can look slender and glamorous."

Expensive shoes often display great craftsmanship, using beautiful leathers and exquisite details and are a pleasure just to hold and look at. Handling them, the sense of possibility is also aroused. What kind of adventure might happen to a woman wearing those shoes that would not be possible otherwise? Less romantically considered, designer shoes are a source of status. It is no secret that women dress primarily to have their efforts appreciated by other women and a few discerning men. Most other men, at best, notice and appreciate the overall effect.

Once-a-Year Clothing

There are certain clothes that we believe we cannot get rid of, either because they were expensive or because they were gifts. They are "perfectly good." Except that when our hand reaches into the closet, for some never-to-be-understood reason, it bypasses them every time. Finally, we force ourselves to wear the outfit—thus circumventing rules such as "If you haven't worn it in a year, give it away." But we don't feel particularly comfortable or happy when we have it on.

Another type of once-a-year clothing is literally that. The Scottish plaid skirt that you wear to the "Robert Burns supper," every January, the Victorian outfit you put on for Heritage Days, the St. Patrick's Day emerald sweater, the Christmas-decorated sweatshirt, and so on. The gingham ruffled skirt your mother gave you that would be perfect for a square dance—if you ever went to square dances.

Borrowed Characteristics

Clothing does not exist in a vacuum; it is not simply a certain amount of fabric and thread. A style has larger connotations that everyone recognizes, though it can also have personal associations known only to ourselves. Camouflage pants signal the drama of the military. An Irish cable-knit sweater evokes wholesomeness and country living and goes well with the tweed jackets and suede elbow patches of the discerning intellectual. When we wear clothing reminiscent of film stars or British spies or Native American culture, we cannot help to take on some of their characteristics.

Other clothes have magical or protective properties that are secret to us. Although we may not consciously know why, we feel safe and happy wearing them. Dale remembers being attached to "a grayish, itchy, oversized sweater" that she wore all the time—to the point where her mother threatened to peel it off her back. She also had a pair of bell bottoms that she decorated with paint, patches, and glittery stones that made her feel like the artist she later became.

It is important to have several pieces of clothing—a necklace, a feather boa, or a leather jacket—that make us feel special when we put them on.

Bargains

You know what these are. Some may even be hanging in your closet with the wonderfully discounted price tags still attached, price tags that made you think, "I can always use a shirt for only $6." Other "bargains" looked good in the dressing room but haven't been seen in that same flattering light since. When you look at your bargains, ask yourself why they hung around the store, unbought, until they went on the sale rack. We love thrift shops, but when something looks almost new, we ask ourselves why the previous owner rarely wore it. There may be a good reason.

The Pain of Transitions

We can run into difficulties downscaling our clothes when we do not feel ready to move on to the next phase of life. Dorothy, the woman who brought 16 feet of hanging clothes to her daughter and son-in-law's home, was feeling this way. As happy as she was to see her grandchildren every day, she was experiencing the loss of the home she had sold and the furniture she and her husband had purchased over the years. Her dressy clothes, the outfits she had worn to see clients, were proof of the full life she had lived and that she wasn't yet ready to see disappear.

People who have to make a change that is not entirely their choice understandably feel this way. A man who is entering an assisted living situation may experience a natural sense of loss in parting with his business suits. By giving up his "important" clothes, he is admitting that a significant part of his life is over. If you are helping an elderly parent or relative make the transition, it is better to encourage them to keep a few representative items. In any case, don't say, "Come on, Dad, you won't need those where *you're* going."

Trophy Clothes

While an expensive dark suit or dressy dress may qualify as trophy clothing, it is usually something more exotic and interesting, clothing you don't wear but can't let go.

"I got this sweater in a tiny village outside Lima."

"This panama hat was my great-grandfather's."

"Even though it's too heavy to wear, this necklace is one-of-a-kind."

"I wore this gown when I went to the Oscars' ceremony."

For now, just identify which items fall into this category. We will give you some ideas of what to do with them later on.

Our Bodies, Ourselves

It's time to tell the truth: Dressing room mirrors are angled so that they add an extra 15 pounds to your body from the waist down. Sorry; just kidding. It only *seems* that way. But enough books have been written on women and their body image to keep us from belaboring the point, except to mention how it relates to what is in our closet. As well as the clothes that we do wear, at least some of the time, there are whole other groups that we don't.

Fantasy clothes. No, not the pink boa. What we mean are the pants that were a little tight right from the beginning. But since the ticket says "Size __," which is your size, they *have* to fit. You're a little bloated right now—all that ice cream— but when you get back to your normal weight, those pants will fit fine. You're going to lost 5 pounds after the holidays anyway.

We've all been there. Perhaps the fantasy items are clothes that fit 10 years ago. Perhaps you've had to go on a medication for your health that causes bloating and weight gain. Whatever the reason, there is no shame in giving away clothes that are now too small or outfits that you wore when you were at your thinnest. Keeping them in your closet will not inspire you to starve yourself, any more than keeping a saxophone in your living room will get you into a band. There is a small possibility of both happening, but the odds are low.

Fallback clothes. These are related to fantasy clothing but are more realistic. Everyone's weight tends to fluctuate, and you need clothes to accommodate temporary changes. But within reason. Not three or four entire wardrobes that push against each other for space. It is better to buy pants with relaxed or elasticized waists and loose-fitting shirt jackets, clothes that have some forgiveness built in and can accommodate fluctuations. There is a vast difference between a formfitting knit dress and a cotton shirtdress with an adjustable belt and fuller skirt. The same is true for men. There are few things less appealing to see on men than a tight T-shirt stretched over a beer belly.

PLUNGING IN

By now, you have realized that scaling down your wardrobe is no simple matter. What complicates the process is not only the meaning the clothes have for you but having to decide on a better direction. You will be judging items on a case-by-case basis but not in the same way most organizing books suggest. To help you, we are going to go step-by-step, the way we would if we came into your home and walked over to your closet. If we make a suggestion that does not apply, just move on to the next.

1. Gather together the following items: Black trash bags, several cardboard cartons, large Post-it notes, and a pen.

2. Go to your main clothes closet, and open the door.

3. Pull out everything that is not on a hanger or neatly on a shelf, and pile it on the bedroom floor. You will be surprised at the number of things in your closet that have nothing to do with clothing.

4. Pick out three outfits that you like—clothes that fit you—and that you wear regularly. If you have room, hang them on one end of the closet rail. Otherwise, drape them carefully over your bed. If you don't have three outfits, you will need to buy them, though not right now. But everyone should have three outfits for each season that they could pack for an unexpected trip with 5 minutes' notice.

5. Next, choose something appropriate that fits to wear to each of the following: a funeral, a New Year's Eve party, a church service, a restaurant with friends. Add them to the first group of three. You may not love everything you picked out for special occasions, but at least you know they are there for you until you get the chance to replace them.

6. Choose a mantra. This is something you will keep repeating to yourself. It is the kind of comment we would make to encourage you if we were there with you. Here are some possibilities:

Almost-right clothing will never *be* right.

As long as there are thrift shops, I won't go naked.

I am worth paying full price.

Keeping too-small clothing is stressful and can ruin my day.

When I get rid of these unwearable clothes, I will feel *really* free.

I want a closet filled only with what I love.

One reason a mantra is so important is because you are going to be hearing plenty of other voices. They will be saying things to you like "You never know when you might need that" or "All it needs is _____" or "This is a waste of time when you could be doing something important!" Ignore everything you hear but your mantra.

7. Work with your clothes while they are hanging in the closet, unless they are packed in so tightly you cannot identify items. In that case, take some of them out; if you have a temporary rack on wheels that you can bring in, hang them there. But leave as many inside as you can. There is nothing that will make you want to run screaming out of the room faster than a mountain of clothes piled ignominiously on your bed.

8. Go through the closet and pull out anything you hate, items you *never* liked, gifts with a subtext, clothes that are too small, anything faded or stained. Remember that you have other clothes you have picked out to wear. Toss the shabby things, and put those that are still wearable in one of the big black bags. Be brave.

9. Go and get a cup of tea or coffee, a glass of wine, or diet soda, and sit down in the living room. While you are taking a break, think about how you want to appear to the world—elegant, stable, creative, a free spirit, romantic, refined, capable, etc. Then return to your closet. Look at each item and remove anything that does not fit this description. If your adjective is "sophisticated," you may decide that the matchstick pleated skirt and scuffed Birkenstock sandals, the kilt and Peter Pan–collar blouse, or the snug T-shirt showing the Teddy Bears' Picnic no longer support the way you want to be.

Don't fall into the trap of feeling that you may want to be all those things at different times. For now, pick one or two adjectives, and put what doesn't support them into bags, to trash or to donate.

10. Ditch the residuals. If you have retired or are working at a different kind of job, chances are you have some clothing that you will never wear again. The chapter on "Finding Good Homes" has suggestions for business clothes, but you have to affirm that your 9-to-5 job is over and let go of the clothing attached to it. There are other lifestyle areas with specific clothing that may now be passé if you are starting a different life: the beaded jumpsuit you wore to discos and the overalls you kept for gardening to name two.

11. Make another sweep through the closet and remove the "bargains," the once-a-year clothes, and everything you feel that isn't *you* anymore. Don't stop to negotiate—just do it.

And then stop. Move the boxes and plastic bags out of the bedroom. You are done for now.

Fine-Tuning

A day or two later, return to the closet, and look at what is left. Besides the outfits that you put to one side to keep in the beginning, there will probably be a fair amount of clothing still hanging in your closet that has escaped the preliminary cut. In a perfect world, these clothes would all be perfect too. None of them would need to be cleaned, hemmed, or paired with something you don't yet own. But if the ones that need work are worth keeping, they should be taken immediately to the cleaners to be cleaned, hemmed, or altered. If they aren't worth the money, then say goodbye.

Sometimes organizers advise their clients to make a list of whatever else they would need to be able to wear a particular shirt, pants, sweater, etc. and then go and buy it. We feel that it depends on how easy the missing piece would be to find. Looking for black pants or a navy blazer may be easier than trying to exactly match a shade of red or green, but even neutral tones come in infinite hues and finishes. Colors in department stores go in and out with the seasons, and the particular shade you need may no longer exist in the retail world. At the least, you need to bring the clothes you already own with you. Otherwise, you run a strong risk of owning *two* pieces of clothing that go with nothing.

Once the clothes that need work before you can wear them again are cleared out, you can turn to the rest.

Analyze This!

Here is where you need the large Post-its. You are going to look at each piece of remaining clothing that you have any ambivalence about, and identify what the sticking points are. Writing down an analysis of each item helps to clarify feelings and helps you make a more objective decision. Pull out the first questionable item, and write down, *Problem*. Halfway down write *Why I'm keeping it anyway*. Here are some examples:

a. Blue cotton blouse

Problem: The material makes it look stiff and baggy.

Why I'm keeping it: I like the floral print. I could always wear it under a sweater.

b. White pants

Problem: They have to be washed and ironed every time I wear them. And right now they're too small.

Why I'm keeping them: They're the only pair of white pants I have, and I'm hoping to be thinner in the summer.

c. Orange turtleneck

Problem: I hate the color, and it doesn't look that good on me.

Why I'm keeping it: It's the only thing I have to wear with my tan blazer, and my kids gave it to me for my birthday.

And so on. When you start to write down the reason for keeping something, and it doesn't sound good enough, put the item in the black bag for charity. Otherwise, keep going. You may find that the process is similar to that of labeling photographs; after a while, you know which to get rid of without writing anything down.

By the time you finish analyzing, you will feel exhausted and sick of your clothes. Take another break. There are still the items piled on the floor that were in your closet and need to find a new home as well as more pleasurable activities waiting that have nothing to do with clothes.

Reevaluating

Come back to the labeled clothes that night or the next day or a week later. You will have developed more perspective and can evaluate them more objectively. You might admit that you *never* wear blouses under sweaters and that the white linen pants are too small and too high maintenance to keep. You may also see different possibilities such as wearing a scarf you love with the orange turtleneck and blazer. If you have tagged an item as a gift, and the giver has seen you wear it once or twice, feel free to let it go—particularly if you dislike the way it looks on you. Remember that your goal is to love and wear everything in your closet.

An alternative to using Post-its is to invite a candid friend or relative over to take a look at what's left, someone who will give you an honest opinion. When you ask, "What about this?" you may hear everything from "That shirt always looks great on you" to "It's fine—if you're going to a hoedown." A lot of times, just a facial expression is enough.

Trophy Clothing Revisited

Remember the items you identified as having special meaning, but were no longer wearable? The secret is that though they do not belong in your closet, they can find new life in other places. For instance . . .

Vintage items. Clothing or accessories that have been in your family—such as your great-grandfather's panama hat or your grandmother's wrinkled kid gloves—can be placed in a shadow box (available at large craft/frame stores such as Michael's) along with a photo of the person, a piece of a document they wrote, and perhaps something that was printed in the newspaper about them. Hung on the wall, it makes a meaningful memorial and is not just a hat or a pair of gloves getting dusty in your closet.

Interesting pieces. Jewelry, antique purses, exotic clothing such as a kimono, robe, or handwoven sweater can be hung on the wall to display it. Buy a brass curtain rod with ends that fit in holders, and slide the rod through the garment's sleeve.

Part of a larger item. When Judi was first married, her grandmother crocheted her a beautiful off-white tablecloth. Over the years, with use, it became stained in several places, and some of the threads unraveled. So Judi cut it down and saved the good part to use as a shawl; now it is a window swag in her bedroom, next to a framed photograph of her grandmother, her mother, and herself as a child.

Another way to save. You can preserve the memory of an item by photographing it, with or without your wearing it. If you have several photographs of past clothing, you can make an album. Think of the fun of getting together with friends and making albums entitled "My Beautiful Wardrobe." You can scan or photocopy old photos of you wearing clothes you enjoyed. If you don't have specific pictures, go to a large library, and photocopy ads and articles from *Life Magazine, Seventeen,* etc.

Write something on the page about what that particular outfit or style meant to you. Not only will you have fun doing it and seeing other people's treasures, your descendants will find it fascinating to see crinolines, saddle shoes, and micro-miniskirts!

A Word about Storage

If you are scaling down, chances are you will not have a walk-in closet. If you don't, consider having a closet system installed or buying one yourself. What you need is to make sure it is configured for your particular wardrobe as far as short clothes, longer items, and shoes. If you are installing it yourself, test to see if it will be sturdy enough not to bend under the weight of heavy clothing.

The more you can compartmentalize smaller items, the easier they will be to handle. Organizing stores sell flexible "honeycomb" dividers in which you can nest socks and underwear. There are hangers with openings that hold a lot of scarves, belts, and ties so that they are visible at a glance.

It is important to have each item visible and not buried under something else. Judi, who wears a lot of turtlenecks, keeps them rolled up like Tootsie Rolls and nestled together in one layer, so she can see all the colors at a glance. Marj, who loves to wear hats, keeps them propped up on champagne bottles on her closet shelf; it looks attractive, keeps them from getting crushed, and lets her see what she has to choose from.

SHOPPING 101

Most people have never been taught how to buy clothes that are right for them and end up with too many near misses. If, after scaling down, you aren't thrilled with what is left, here are some suggestions on how to shop intelligently for new clothes, based on what has been helpful to our clients and ourselves.

Have your colors redone. In the 1980s, many people either went to "Color Me Beautiful" studios or learned about it from their friends. Everyone exorcized the "bad" colors from their wardrobes and went shopping with color swatches for their season. It might be a good idea to have a new session, particularly if your hair color has changed since then. At the least, you can look at the book, *Color Me Beautiful*, and review what you have already learned.

Narrow your options. Elaine St. James, author of the charming book, *Simplify Your Life,* has narrowed her color palette down to black. All her clothing is black, though she accessorizes with other colors. A drastic solution, perhaps, but workable for her.

Use a personal shopper. Some department stores still offer this service or can refer you to someone who specializes in helping people put together wardrobes. Our friend, Carole, was very satisfied when she paid a talented

TAMING YOUR NEW WARDROBE

How do you keep from finding yourself in the same position again? Well, for one thing, you are now far more attuned to scaling down and keeping clothing under control. What was in your closet(s) probably took you years to accumulate, years of not worrying about whether or not you had room. You happily shoved items in, especially if you had a walk-in closet that seemed to have endless room.

If you begin shopping more intelligently, you will also need to remember the basic rule, "One in, one out." Don't just remember it, actually recycle something when you buy a new one in the same category, and you will do fine.

---

acquaintance to go shopping with her and help her choose items that both coordinated and were becoming.

Look "at" clothes, rather than shop "for" them. Another friend, Lee, who is always beautifully dressed and teaches groups and individuals how to accessorize, depends on serendipity. Rather than putting herself under the pressure of having to find a particular outfit *now,* when she has time, she browses around stores and buys the perfect items when she finds them. She is experienced enough not to make impulse purchases; but like everything else, it was a lesson she had to learn.

Learn from a book. While you can get an idea from fashion magazines, there are down-to-earth books that can be helpful in teaching you how to focus on and buy the right clothing. They can be found in any library or bookstore. A favorite of ours is *Brenda's Wardrobe Companion* by Brenda Kinsel, a collection of practical suggestions and easily grasped ideas.

Just say no. Women especially are often offered clothing by their mothers, aunts, and other relatives. "I only wore this once; why don't you take it?" In the first place, it was not bought for you; it was purchased to look attractive on someone else. If you don't want to seem churlish, take it home and try it on. If it isn't exactly right—no matter how much it cost—say no to it before it ever gets to your closet.

part 3
SPECIAL SITUATIONS

*"There's lots of things in my life
I absolutely needed to put in, and now there's lots of things
in my life I absolutely need to get out."*

7

CLEARING OUT YOUR FAMILY HOME

For 3 years, the McMann home sat on a corner lot, furnished down to the flour in the canisters and the sheets on the beds—but eerily still. The neighbors were restless and starting to complain. Although one of the sons stopped by to mow the lawn and pick up the circulars left in the driveway, the flower beds were weedy and overgrown. Wooden window frames had started to peel; the house gave the feeling of being abandoned.

The decision about what to do with the house had polarized the McMann children. Nell, the oldest daughter, felt strongly that they should just clear out the contents and sell it. She had begun referring to it as the "House of Usher." Pat, the younger son, insisted that it was disrespectful to dispose of their parents' things and home while their mother was still living, even though she was in an "Alzheimer's Neighborhood" in an assisted care facility. He was also not ready to let the house where he had grown up go to strangers. The other two children agreed with Nell but were not ready for a showdown. Meanwhile Nell and her sister had started quietly removing items "for safekeeping."

Although it is easy to say what they should have done, making decisions about the family home can be a difficult and emotional process. When the situation arises, families are rarely prepared. Even when parents move into interim housing such as a condominium or senior community, there is still the question of how to divide and dispose of their belongings—as well as when to do it. In the case of the McMann family, the will stipulated dividing the estate equally among all four children but did not mention personal belongings or furniture.

Up to this point in the book, we have been addressing people who are able to scale down and make choices themselves. This chapter is directed toward those who have to clear out the homes of elderly relatives, either through death or because the person needs to be moved to an assisted living facility. We are writing about situations in which the parent or older relative/friend is not able to take an active role in the process. Because of longer life spans, you can end up trying to move and scale down yourself while simultaneously having to handle the same situation with an elderly parent.

MAKING A DIFFICULT TRANSITION A LITTLE EASIER

The transition to an assisted living facility is often complicated by the fact that the older adult is not willing to go. Even if on some level, they can understand the necessity of moving, they refuse to be a willing participant. They may deny that they are going *anywhere* and will not cooperate by selecting what they want to bring with them.

No one needs to be reminded that we are living in a transitional time. We have been able to improve physical life expectancy through medical research and treatment but have not been as successful in finding cures for mental conditions such as dementia brought on by ministrokes and Alzheimer's disease. Judi considers her family representative of these changes. All four of her grandparents were living at home when they died in their eighties of cancer or a stroke. Given these examples, her own parents lived as if they would never become incapacitated. But her father was diagnosed with a brain tumor at 84 and never recovered, and her mother suffered a series of brief blackouts, probably small strokes, and became more and more confused. It was unsafe for her to live alone in a large house; even daily calls or visits by her children were not enough.

Horror Story #1

A move to a nursing home was necessary for Dr. George Matthews, an English professor who was retired from a well-regarded university. He could no longer get in and out of bed by himself and needed full-time medical supervision. Both of his children lived at a distance and were unable to make the sacrifices his full-time care would have demanded. In the past, when they had urged him to move closer to where they lived, Dr. Matthews had refused to leave his beloved milieu. Now he no longer had a choice.

In their haste to have their father situated and properly cared for, Todd and Janice packed just what he would need in two suitcases and bundled him off to the facility. They made arrangements to have the contents of his apartment placed in storage—he owned many valuable volumes and pieces of art—then flew back to their own homes, reassured that he was receiving the best care.

Todd and Janice did the right thing—but failed miserably in empathy. Not only was their father in a strange place, there was no sign of his beloved books and journals, pictures of his deceased wife and his family, keepsakes from his years of teaching and travel—not even a favorite lamp. His children had not thought to transfer his newspaper subscription, so he could no longer even do the crossword puzzle. Blaming them for "stealing my stuff," he refused to speak to Todd and Janice on the phone when they called. Without the stimulation he had been dependent on, he lapsed quickly into confusion.

When it became necessary to place her in a suite in a supervised living facility, her children made sure that she had her favorite pieces of furniture, paintings, and photographs, several bisque dolls from her collection, her canaries, and Max, her wire-haired terrier. As mentioned in the chapter "Finding Good Homes," she soon lost interest in the pets; they were adopted by staff members. It was painful to see the valuable dolls deteriorate through careless treatment; but, after all, they were *hers*. At the time she was moved, she was able to recognize familiar items but was not able to choose what to bring with her. It was therefore crucial to select items that would help her continue to be who she was as much as possible, belongings from her home that reflected her essence.

What if you are helping a parent who is still able to make decisions about his or her move? As with Judi's mother and the dolls, you need to remember whose belongings these are. If your father wants to sell the antique furniture at auction and give the proceeds to the Boy Scouts of America or his church or his broker, that is his choice. You might ask for one or two pieces that have special meaning for you, but it is not your prerogative to try to talk him out of his plan. Your purpose is to help him move happily from a large space to a smaller one, not make decisions for him.

If he seems unwilling to deal with his possessions, you can ask questions such as "What are you thinking about doing with your piano/war memorabilia/stamp collection?" You may get answers ranging from "I'd like to keep it in the family" to "You can sell it and pay for college expenses" or "I can't think about that *now.*" Most of us are uncomfortable being put on the spot. We prefer to have time to process and mull things over. Even if you get a nonanswer, he may mention what he wants a few days or weeks later, suddenly bringing it up as if it were his own idea.

When Sam's mother moved to assisted living, she selected the facility and picked out her room. Yet she asked him to "keep my furniture until I find an apartment again." Rather than point out that she would never again be living on her own, he agreed and placed the contents of her condominium in storage. When she died several months later, Sam and his sister took what was meaningful to them from the storage unit and disposed of the rest with care.

Collecting Crucial Information

It is beyond the scope of this book to detail the emotional interactions that help a parent move into assisted living or make other decisions. Situations vary widely. Some older adults, such as Judi's parents, believe they will never die and are not receptive to planning beyond having a current will. Others, such as her mother-in-law, Muriel, take the initiative in making a DNR (Do Not Resuscitate order) and end-of-life directive. Muriel had a prepaid burial plan and had even written down the selections she wanted read and the classical music she wanted played at her memorial service. Her family joked that even at the end, she was trying to educate people. When she died at 94, all her sons needed to do was bake a selection of her wonderful cookies, tarts, and breads for the reception after the service.

Marj took the initiative with her daughter, Angelyn, and son-in-law, Dave, to sit down and discuss the topics that every child or heir needs to know. (See below.) They all felt relieved and affirmed afterward. But if your parents or older relatives do not broach the subject themselves, you will need to do so. It sometimes helps to start with a disclaimer, such as "I know we won't need this information for a long time, but it's good to get it out of the way." There *will* be a sense of relief afterward that such "taboo" topics have been openly aired.

What do you need to find out from your parents or tell your children?

- The location of the will and if it is current. A copy should be with the executor, formerly the family lawyer, now often one of the children. On asking, Paul found that his parents had not made a will since he was a baby, though several more children had been born. Though his parents insisted that they had "plenty of time," he was instrumental in helping them have a more equitable will drawn up.

- Any DNR orders and other end-of-life directives. These should be discussed by the parents with their doctor, so that they understand just what they are choosing. Make sure that the conditions are clearly spelled out.

- Whether or not they want to donate any of their organs.

- The location of military discharge papers, so that they can be interred in a military cemetery if that is what they wish. When Marj was helping one of her older boarding school teachers get resettled, she realized that Mary had served as a WAC in World War II. Marj located Mary's discharge papers and found that Mary was eligible for a number of benefits, including interment and a headstone. Spouses of servicemen and servicewomen are eligible for burial in military cemeteries as well.

- The location of insurance policies, bank accounts, and the key to a safe deposit box if there is one.

• Any hiding places they use for money and valuables. Often people like to have some cash on hand or jewelry that they enjoy wearing but want to keep safe. We've heard about valuables stowed at the bottom of shoe bag pockets or at the bottom of a hamper under dirty clothes, money kept in a Bible or in a hollow book resembling a real one. If you are clearing out a relative's home, check everything from coat pockets to piles of plastic bags.

Getting Outside Help

Sometimes it is necessary to bring in an intermediary, a person who is not part of the family. An older relative may respond better to someone who is closer to them in age or does not have, to their thinking, an ulterior motive. When parents are in their prime, they sometimes extract promises from their children that "you'll never put me in one of those homes." If it later becomes necessary, someone objective can help get past the "you *promised*" impasse.

The older adult may be able to direct what happens to their possessions but may not have the physical strength to complete the process themselves. In cases where a child or younger relative is not able to help them—or the parent does not want them involved for fear they will "throw everything away"—an outside helper is appropriate. This does not always have to be a professional. If friends or church members are anxious to help out, working with someone they know can be very reassuring.

If such a person is not available, where can you find help? Most social service agencies that are run by the county or the city have "Adult Services." If they cannot help you directly, they will refer you to community resources. Local AARP groups and attorneys who specialize in elder care can make recommendations as well. Professional organizers in your area can be contacted by calling the National Association of Professional Organizers (NAPO) at 512-206-0151 or looking on the Internet at www.napo.net.

It is sad to hear about people hiring removal companies to come in and simply trash everything. Who knows what gems and family memories are being hauled off to the dump? On the other hand, we can understand the homeowners' or heirs' desperation. Sometimes a look at floor-to-ceiling stacks is all it takes to send them screaming out the door. And people's lives *are* more important than things. But if you have the time and stamina, sorting through the home yourself is the better way to go.

UNDERSTANDING YOUR FAMILY DYNAMICS

Ultimately, you and your family will need to agree to some kind of fair and equitable way to distribute the possessions that your parents have accumulated. But before you try to find a distribution method that everyone considers fair enough to participate in, realize that there are complicated emotions at play. Old insecurities breed fears of "I won't get what I want—as usual." The belongings to be divided are imbued with memories and emotions and will not be seen objectively. If you feel a sibling or cousin is taking too much, your sense of rivalry will kick in and can make you reach for more than you want or need. There is also the knowledge that this is a one-time opportunity, and if you don't take what you want now, there will be no further chance to do so. This fear can make you end up taking more than you have room for, just to be safe.

Your family may also have different ideas of what is "fair."

"I live the closest and helped them out, so I should have first consideration."

"Dad promised me his workbench and tools."

"I'm the only girl, so I should get Mom's jewelry."

"A lot of those antiques were gifts from us, so we should get those back before we divide the rest up."

"You guys already have houses; I have to move out of this house and furnish my own apartment!"

"I only want one thing—the painting of the family over the mantel."

"They helped you out financially; that has to factor in."

"The things that my parents had before my father married your mother should be off-limits."

Whew! While some of these claims may have merit, unless everyone agrees to honor them, it is unlikely that they will prevail. Barbara and Sally, two friends of ours, came from out of town to help close up the family home when their mother moved in with their brother and his wife, Esther. Brad and Esther had been the main caretakers for their father as well, though he had continued to live in the family home. Brad was at work when the three women went through the house. "We'll take this," Esther said, pointing to the dining room buffet. "I've always wanted the fireplace set," she went on as they moved into the living room. Her claims continued throughout the home. Barbara managed to get the family Bible, and Sally the handbuilt dollhouse from her father, though Esther looked a little put out at that.

Back at the hotel, Sally broke the silence. "I'm so mad I could spit!"

"You could?" Barbara looked relieved. "I felt like that too at the house but was ashamed to admit it."

"And she's only the daughter-in-law!"

"I know. But she's married to Brad. And look how much they've done for the folks. Besides, if having the things means that much to her . . ."

Sally wasn't convinced.

They talked about it more over dinner and finally decided that it was not important enough to cause a family rupture. After all, they had each gotten something they valued and could live without the rest of the stuff. Esther had done as much for their parents as any daughter would have. Once they had released their feelings by discussing them, they went back to loving her as much as always.

This was one family's solution. It may not be yours. As Richard, a client of Marj's, pointed out in a similar situation, his sister had also reaped benefits—babysitting, home construction help, hand-me-downs, and informal gifts—by living close to their parents. He was not ready to abrogate things that were meaningful to him.

Further Complications

There is no question that families are complicated, especially when the families are "blended" and seem to have differing levels of claims. Even if the parents have left a fair will dividing money and real estate, what is considered "non-titled property"—furniture, dishes, collections, jewelry, books, photographs, tools, and similar items—is usually not mentioned.

When Lynn told us about bringing her deceased stepmother's sisters over to look through the household and take what they wanted—her own father had died 2 years earlier—she sounded put out. As the executor of the will and the only child who lived locally, it fell to her to transport the items they wanted to their homes.

We asked her how she had divided things up.

"First my children, my husband, and I went in and took what we wanted, then I contacted her sons, and they came with their families. Her sisters came over after that."

Was this a fair method of division? You decide.

THE CLEANUP

When Judi and her brothers were doing a preliminary clearing out of their parents' house after it had been unlived in for several months, they rented the largest dumpster available. They filled it completely one Saturday morning with discards from the garage and the basement. People visiting their parents' warm and beautifully decorated home would have had little idea that such pack rat tendencies were at work.

The unseen storage areas told another story. Their father saved everything and had hundreds of glass jars on his workbench filled with mysterious metal parts. Their mother was more selective, but if she no longer wanted to display something or was given a gift she could not use, she blithely consigned it to the large basement. The antique auctions to which they were addicted were a temptation they could not overcome. If the price was right, they brought it home, often in pieces.

Five adults and several children worked at the job, putting aside things that still had value and putting items that were "still good" but that no one would want in the future by the curb: Step stools, worn outdoor furniture, sawhorses, a lot of molded plastic were carried outside. One man in particular scooped items up as fast as they appeared. The lure of the free . . .

A lot of dust was stirred up—as well as many emotions. Judi had the fantasy that her terminally ill father, miraculously recovered, would stride up the driveway and demand, "What are you *doing*? Who said you could throw my things away?" (She knew that her mother, if equally recovered, would not care).

Her brother complained that his wife was being "insensitive" when she treated the treasures of his boyhood too lightly. One of the grandchildren sat on the living room couch and wept because he would never again come to the house on holidays and have his beloved grandparents waiting for him. Various basement items evoked nostalgia and sadness in different family members as well as helpless laughter.

When they had finished decluttering, they went out to lunch and spent several hours reminiscing about their family and happier times. At the end of the day, they felt at peace. Dividing up and disposing of the rest of the things would come later, when everyone felt ready. But this was a sad but necessary beginning, and it helped that they had done it together.

How Much Time Is Enough?

Back to the McMann family we met at the beginning of the chapter. They had reached an impasse about what to do with their parents' home. Leaving a house with all its contents inside—vulnerable to decay, theft, and fire—is not optimal. Many insurance companies will drop their coverage if they know that a home is untenanted. In this situation, the disgruntled neighbors would have forced the issue, had not the stock market taken a downswing. Mrs. McMann was supported in the nursing home by dividends and annuities, and it was necessary to sell the house to maintain the high cost of her care. Because it would benefit his mother, Pat, the holdout, agreed that clearing out the home had to be done.

There is an opposite danger as well. Acting too hastily, taking action before a plan has been agreed upon and everyone is on board can create rifts that never fully heal. In most families, there is a take-charge contingent that wants to get everything settled and done with. If this describes you, slow down. In a situation where so much emotion is involved, and the threat of misunderstanding is so high, the process must be a deliberate one.

MAKING A DISTRIBUTION PLAN

The first step is to communicate with everyone involved. If this is your family home, make sure that your siblings are contacted and involved in every step. If

Horror Story #2

At the end of one of our workshops, Anna came up to us, close to tears. Her husband had died the year before, and her daughter-in-law was insisting that they clear out his clothes and personal belongings. Now. When the family got together for Mother's Day, Joanne had been ready to roll. She insisted her husband, brother-in-law, and Anna come upstairs and get started on the closet. "My younger son got so upset that he walked out and didn't come back," Anna sobbed. "Nothing got done, and the day was ruined. I'm afraid it's going to keep happening."

"But your sons don't have to be there," we told her. "Not if it's too upsetting for them."

"Really?" It was a revelation.

"You and Joanne can do it yourselves. If you're giving the clothes to charity, just set aside two or three items that may have some sentiment attached to them: a favorite leather jacket or sweatshirt, maybe a watch or cufflinks, and offer them to your sons. But there are certain tasks that some people just can't handle, and they shouldn't be forced to do them."

Anna looked a whole lot happier. "I'll do it myself then," she said firmly. "I know that's what my husband would have wanted."

In defense of Joanne, who was related to the family by marriage and perhaps saw the situation more objectively, she may have felt that the family was stuck and could not move on until this step was taken. But she was mistaken to feel that every family member had to be forced to participate. And she had a disastrous sense of timing.

the house or apartment belonged to a childless aunt or uncle or grandparents, involve your cousins as well as your siblings. Even if you think it is going to slow down the process or complicate things. Even if some of them live at a distance. Each relative has the right to be involved; perhaps the process *needs* to be slowed down. Certainly before you begin taking items from the house, wait until everyone has agreed on a method and a time to gather to do so.

Siblings or cousins who say, "I don't want anything," should not be taken at face value and written out of the process. First, explore what they are really saying. Perhaps they see it as "dividing up the spoils," and it feels ghoulish to them. Perhaps they are still grieving and imagine it would be too painful. Even if you've talked to them at length, and they are adamant, we suggest setting aside one or two family treasures to offer to them and certainly any of their personal belongings. They can always say no.

Horror Story #3

After her mother's funeral, when family and friends came back to the house, Virginia went upstairs to her parents' old bedroom. She was shocked to see that her mother's jewelry box had been ransacked. "Literally everything of value or sentimental meaning was gone."

Five years later, she was still seething. "My sister-in-law and her daughters had gone there straight from the hospital and helped themselves to whatever they wanted. When I confronted her, she was very nice about it. She said, 'Since you only have boys, I didn't think you'd be interested.' I told her I *was* interested, and she promised to give me some of the jewelry. She never has. I've never felt the same toward my nieces either."

What's wrong with this picture, other than the fact that Virginia has a boorish sister-in-law who probably violated the terms of the will while she was at it? What's wrong is that both women let stuff take the ascendancy over family relationships. In the end, jewelry is only metal and stone and does not retain the spirit of its former owner. You can touch your grandfather's pocket watch or your mother's engagement ring and feel the warmth of memory, but you can feel the same by looking at a favorite photo.

The injustice, the unfairness, rankle Virginia just as much as their greed and their indifference about what her mother's things meant to her. But if she can go back to feeling loving toward her nieces, being interested in their lives, and even enjoying her sister-in-law for their shared experience, it would enrich her own life. Ironically, once warm relationships were re-established, she might be offered some of her mother's jewelry. And by then, Virginia might find that it does not matter as much.

Deciding What Is Important

In Virginia's situation (See Horror Story #3 on page 103), what her sister-in-law did was unforgivable. And Virginia did not forgive her. But in their case, resentments and rivalries had been building between them for years; what happened with the jewelry was the climax, not the beginning. It was sad that the nieces and nephews were caught in the crossfire. If relationships with your siblings or cousins are less than ideal, it may be necessary to decide on formal guidelines. A godsend in this area is the workbook, "Who Gets Grandma's Yellow Pie Plate?" (Available from the University of Minnesota, www.yellowpieplate.umn.edu or 800-876-8636 for $12.50 plus shipping). It gives examples of family complications and has detailed lists to complete and questions to answer, both for older family members while they are still able to make decisions and for the surviving heirs.

If family harmony is your main priority, and family members feel close to one another—or at least not in open conflict—you can reassure each other that "no 'stuff' is as important as our relationship." If you keep that as your family mantra, it will take you far.

But there will still be decisions to be made. In our experience, quality is more important to most people than quantity. So we would suggest that everyone involved in the process write down the two items from the family home that they would most like to have. If only the children or direct cousins will be participating in the division of items, they can ask their spouses and children to do the same and bring their requests along.

The diversity of desires will surprise you. In our experience, everyone has been able to get at least one of the two things they wanted and often both. When two or more people ask for the same thing, there can be discussion about it, including whether or not the other item on their list is available. But if everyone gets at least one thing that represents family and continuity to them, they seem more relaxed about the rest of the process.

After the primary items are chosen, you may want to continue by picking a method (e.g., drawing straws, youngest to oldest etc.) and continue to select, in turn, other items you would like to have. But stop when you have all you really want or need, even if the process continues.

Stumbling Blocks

Even when you have a method of distribution that everyone agrees is fair, or fair enough, you still need to deal with your own feelings. What we have seen in ourselves and others are several different pitfalls:

"I can always use this." The odd thing is that we often pass up furniture and more interesting items for the mundane. Everyone is able to resist a decorative pillow or umbrella stand but fights to have a cookie sheet or travel alarm clock. We know which of the larger items won't fit with our decor, but who can resist an extra paring knife? Be very careful about duplicates; they are useful, they are free, and they will add to your clutter.

"He's getting more than I am!" This usually happens after everyone has gotten the items they truly want, and the other things are being divided up and disposed of. You have a few meaningful objects chosen, and you know where you are going to put them in your home. You feel content that you are keeping what your parents or relatives would have wanted you to have to honor their memory and have gotten something for your spouse and children as well. Then you notice a sibling or cousin stockpiling a large collection of stuff, and ancient rivalries kick in.

The worst thing you can do is jump back in, and start grabbing. Take a break and go outside or into another room. Remove yourself physically from the scene and remind yourself that you are an adult, and your needs have been met. They are the ones who will have to find storage space for all those things at the end of the day. Once you have your family treasures installed in your home, the memory of the things you didn't take will fade quickly.

"It's one of a kind." Inevitably, there will be valuable objects that cannot be duplicated. The painting of the family over the mantel, which we mentioned before. The grandfather clock that has been in the family for generations. Mom's diamond engagement ring. The illustrated book of Bible stories that was read to each child in turn. If there are enough of these items for each heir to have one, they can be divided by the usual process. But often there are only one or two things that are truly unique and which several people are interested in having.

If they are portable, you may want to consider passing them around, having a designated time everyone is together, such as the holidays, to pass them on. If they are not portable, such as a piano or grandpa's rolltop desk, consider an arbitrary method such as drawing names or straws. That eliminates the ill feelings caused by statements that begin, "I should really have it because . . ."

In Judi's family, there were three items that, though no one's first choice, were one of a kind. It was decided that each child should take one of them for a year, then pass it on to one of the others. These were their mother's solid gold charm bracelet, a large piece of scrimshaw on ivory, and a third item that Judi cannot for the life of her remember. But this is often what happens. Things that seemed very desirable in the emotion of the moment gradually become just another bit of stuff.

"It seems disrespectful to get rid of any of my family's things." This feeling is not uncommon, especially when a beloved parent or grandparent has just died, and you are the main beneficiary. Even if you know that everything was not sacred to them, items can seem supercharged with emotion. If you have the room to do so, pack everything in cartons, and put the boxes away for several months. Then, when you feel more ready, give them a quick going-through to remove anything flawed or which you can't remember them using. Also remove any heirloom or sentimental items that you want to display.

You will feel a sense of accomplishment for having gotten through any of the process. It may take you several times over a few months to be able to make decisions on giving away usable items. But as time goes on, you will start to see a lot of things as just "stuff" and be able to separate out what is truly representative of the person. Although that may sound harsh, it is what happens. As we said earlier in the book, it is not disrespectful to their memory if their belongings can now bless someone else.

"How can I get rid of something I know they loved or was specifically willed to me?" It is one thing to give kitchen items, linens, or clothing to charity. It is harder to give something away that you know they valued, even if you don't feel the same way about the item. One of our favorite examples is of our friend Pam, whose mother's whatnot cabinets sat for several years in her basement because she could neither bring herself to use them with her decor nor dispose of them. Finally, she brought them to a local antiques shop and placed them on consignment. When they sold, she used the proceeds to plant a beautiful perennial garden in her backyard. Her English mother had loved gardening; now whenever Pam looks out her window at the shrubs and flowers, she is reminded of their close relationship.

A Last Bit of Advice

Since many of the memories and feelings evoked in this process will go back to childhood, it is instructive to realize that all we need to know to get through it, we learned back then:

Play fair.
Take your turn.
Don't be greedy and grab things.
Finish your work.
Be kind.
Don't hurt people's feelings.
Friends are more important than toys.
If you substitute family relationships for the last rule, you will do fine.

8

YOUR CUISINART OR MINE?

When many of us were young, the custom was to get married right after high school or college. We brought relatively little to the marriage: clothes, books, childhood curios, some hand-me-down family furniture, and an assortment of wedding presents. Together, we bought a few large items such as a bed and a dining room set. But in those days, real men did not worry about throw pillows, and the kitchen was used for grilling hamburgers and heating formula. Gourmet cooking meant cooking Italian. Judi and her friends proudly served the identical meal to each other—veal parmigiana, butternut squash baked with brown sugar, and ice cream with hot fudge sauce. Marj and her husband were teaching at a boarding school and didn't have to cook at all.

But times change. People are now marrying later. A common trend, after college, is to thoroughly furnish an apartment or even to buy a condo or house. Many people enter marriage or a committed relationship with a lot of stuff and preferences. Besides marriage, there are gay partnerships, Golden Girls' arrangements, siblings deciding to live together after being widowed, and second or third marriages. A couch picked out by an ex-wife comes with more than just cushions.

Blending two households into one has many of the same elements as moving into a smaller space. The process involves compromise, paring down, and trying to create a new environment. There are differences, however, a different dynamic at work.

FIRST TIMERS

The saving grace among young couples who decide to marry or live together is that their love and optimism for the future creates a playing field of good will. Besides items that they have purchased new, they may also have a number of curb finds, thrift store purchases, and hand-me-downs to which they are not overly attached. The sticking points are often minor, but emotion-based. They can present the need for diplomatic ways to find compromise. After all, criticism of my *Casablanca* poster is a criticism of *me*. It is easy, once things get personal, for the process to deteriorate into a power struggle as accusations are lobbed like grenades:

"You have so many frilly pillows, I can't find the bed."

"That leather chair was nice once—before your dog ate it."

"I don't want *The Three Stooges* in *my* bedroom."

"Whoever heard of a beer safe?"

"That fuzzy toilet seat cover has got to go."

"A beach towel tacked over the window is not my idea of curtains."

And those are minor points, compared with some of the others:

"I like clean lines. I can't take all these knickknacks!"

"That glass and chrome dining table set looks so *cold.*"

"We can't fit four dressers into the bedroom, but they all have stuff we need."

"My grandparents bought that Formica kitchen table when they first got married, and I'm not giving it up."

"Your clothes take up the whole closet!"

"The waterbed was the first piece of furniture I ever bought—and I still think it's cool."

"I want a living room, not a sports arena!"

Speaking of sports arenas, when Dominick and Susan got engaged at 34, it made sense for them to live in the townhouse he had purchased 2 years earlier. The space was much larger than Susan's apartment, and there was even a room that was still unfurnished. Susan was looking forward to using it as a home office and, eventually, a nursery, and Dominick was happy to relinquish it. What he was unwilling to do, however, was make any changes in his living room.

Dominick was proud of his living room, which was the room you saw first when you came through the door. It had a plasma TV, black vinyl couches that made him think of leather, and lots of electronics equipment against the walls. A large Foosball table was right next to the window. He and his friends loved hanging out there, and his home was the favorite site for Super Bowl parties. It would have worked out nicely if Susan were as interested in sports as he was— but she wasn't. Her suggestion that once they were married, he could move his media center up to the family room met with no enthusiasm.

"Short of strapping that huge TV to my back and crawling up the stairs, there was nothing I could do," Susan told us. She decided, wisely, not to press the issue. Instead, *she* took the family room on the next level and made it into a gracious living room/dining area where she could entertain friends and have romantic dinners with Dominick. "When we move to a house, I'll have an equal say. I don't think he cares if he's in the front room or not as long as he has plenty of space for his stuff."

Three Unscientific Principles

We feel Susan's decision was a wise one, based on three truths we have observed:

1. Rooms are not preordained to be used for specific purposes, especially if they have already been furnished another way. If you are an artist, and the best light and largest windows are in what would normally be the dining room, find somewhere else to eat. If a small back room has the best view, one you would like to wake up to, enlarge the windows if necessary, and make that the "master bedroom."

2. Many men resist any change to their physical environment. This is not a sexist statement; it is a fact of life. How many men feel that rearranging the living room is the perfect way to spend a free afternoon? But it goes deeper than that. When

Judi's friends Dawn and Eileen spent the day rearranging the furniture in Eileen's house in accordance with Feng Shui principles, then added some candles and crystals, her husband, Brad, came home that night and went ballistic. He had spent a hard day on the planning board and was not prepared to find himself in an unfamiliar environment. He demanded that everything be restored to its original place.

It is true that he'd had no say in the rearranging. But as Eileen pointed out, not once in many years of marriage had she suggested making a style change and had Brad say, "Wow, what a great idea. Let's do it!" The best she could elicit was a cautious "It's a possibility." His normal response was "Why? It looks fine the way it is."

3. When you move into someone else's space, an environment in which they have already been living, don't expect to make dramatic changes. They have arranged things, over time, to suit themselves, and although they want to compromise, it won't be easy for them. There may be pleasure in merging two collections of books or CDs and upgrading kitchen appliances, but there is rarely equality of furnishings—or closet space, especially if the woman has been there first. A lot of men have found themselves getting dressed in another bedroom—the only place where their clothes can fit.

If you are moving in, expect to keep a few pieces of furniture to which you are especially attached, and discard the rest. The laws of equality do not work out here.

One woman who had antique furniture she had collected put it in storage until they could move from his apartment into a house. They agreed that when that happened, his high-tech look would get toned down.

"EITHER THAT WALLPAPER GOES, OR I DO"

Although those are purported to be Oscar Wilde's dying words, their sentiment has been echoed as people try to blend two households, especially when they are older. When Felix took a good look at his fiancée's bedroom after they decided that they would live in her apartment, he took note of the ruffled curtains and lavender bedspread, white wicker furniture, and prints of old-fashioned children and declared, "I couldn't live in this room."

And he didn't. Anne thought he would come around. She wasn't willing to give up a setting that she had dreamed of since childhood, which her parents had never been able to afford. *His* bedroom, she said scornfully, looked like it had escaped from the zoo. The furniture was all chrome, with large wall prints of wild animals and a leopard-skin coverlet.

There turned out to be other things that neither wanted to compromise on, and they decided to continue as "steady dates" rather than man and wife.

"Don't Touch That Painting!"

In situations where one or both people have been married before, moving into a home that was shared with a former partner is a delicate matter. In this instance, divorce can be preferable to widowhood or widowerhood, because it usually comes with less sentimental baggage. That is, if you marry a widower and move into his home, you may experience the double whammy of his not wanting his environment disturbed and of his feeling disloyal to his deceased wife by making changes to their former home. It takes a secure new wife not to be troubled by the wedding photograph of the original couple that seems rooted to his bedside table. It may be hard enough to look out the back window and see the collection of bird feeders and birdhouses with the sign that reads "Gloriann's Garden"—when you're not Gloriann.

This is not to say that all widows are sensitive and all widowers oblivious. There have been enough stories about "sainted first husbands" to lay that idea to rest. But because women have traditionally been given the responsibility of creating the physical environment, they are usually more sensitive to its nuances. Most widows in that situation would stow the old photograph or move it to a more neutral place. The past must be validated and recognized—but not at the expense of the current relationship.

If you are the partner moving into the home, suggest changes gradually. When you can change a room's focus or motif by deciding how you both want it to be, as we discuss in the chapter "Have It Your Way," it will feel more natural.

What we have been discussing does not even include the complications of either partner's children, whether they are grown or not. The problem is stated well in the book, *Unmarried to Each Other.*

"Beyond simply finding room for that weightlifting equipment, space has meaning. One of the hardest things for Marion to handle was her partner's request to use her son's bedroom as a work space: 'Even though my son is now almost 30 and on his own for many years, that room still felt like his room, his special place where he would return on a visit back home. Making the transition was not only a physical change but also an emotional one for all involved.'"

The best option, of course, is to move to a new space when you marry—even if it is not the most "practical." If beginning your new life in a neutral setting is not possible, discuss sensitive areas *before* you get married. If the stuffed African animal heads from her deceased husband's family make you queasy, tell your fiancée that before the wedding. It may be that she never cared for them, either, but didn't realize she *could* take them down.

Although you will be bringing along some of your own furniture, purchasing a new bed together is crucial. Even if it isn't "practical." Especially if the existing bed is a valuable antique passed down from the deceased spouse's family. The past must be recognized and respected, but so must the present.

Guidelines for Blending

Back to the situation of merging two households. It helps to recognize certain truths:

1. Each person thinks that many of the other person's things would be a perfect contribution to a yard sale. "Stuff" is so complicated that we often don't understand why a particular item inspired someone we are close to. Even when we do understand, it doesn't mean that we would choose to share our lives with a taped-up leather recliner or the complete set of *Wizard of Oz* figurines, down to 40 Munchkins. Think about your friends' homes. You may admire them and think that they "work" but would resist the idea of having to move into them yourself. They are not to your particular taste.

2. When you are blending two households, try to understand that *you* are not being rejected even if some of your choices are. The other person needs to be reminded of that as well.

3. It is helpful to know *why* something is being saved. As Marj points out from personal experience, "The ugliest footstool in the world may be the only thing left from a grandparent." Ask questions about items with which you do not want to share space. "When did you get this? Does it mean a lot to you?" You may see certain items in a new way. If your partner doesn't ask, volunteer information about whatever is particularly meaningful to you.

4. Too much compromise pleases no one. That is, "dumbing down" a room until there is no longer anything offensive in it but nothing exciting either won't make anyone happy. If your tastes are seriously different, it is better to each have a room that you decorate and express your tastes in, and find a third style you can both agree on for the other rooms. There will be some common ground, if only because more colors, furniture pieces, and accessories than you might imagine can fit very different styles.

London antiques dealer, Robert Kenally, was a "maximalist" who collected everything that interested him, from Staffordshire dogs to mannequin heads to Victorian fabrics. He especially enjoyed the lush look of displaying them all at once. His partner, David Wu, was a painter who was happiest in stark black and white rooms and a kitchen with bare countertops. Their drawing room and library reflected Robert's dream, but the minimalist kitchen and dining room were what David wanted. They lived together in harmony with spaces each of them loved until Robert, who was older, passed on, and David drastically decluttered.

A TV program called *Merge* jumps into situations where the couples are stalemated, taking liberties that only a third-person television show is allowed. Each party is able to "protect" one item that they cannot live without; they write down what it is, and slip it to the decorating team. Literally everything else in the two households is fair game—to be used, recycled into a new piece, donated to charity, or tossed into the dreaded compactor. The payoff is that the couple ends up with a beautifully decorated space containing the best belongings of each. A luxury item or two, added by the decorators, enhances the process.

WHO GETS THE COMPUTER AFTER THE DIVORCE?

If you pick up one of the hundreds of books that have been written about divorce, you will find every aspect discussed at length—except for the division of "stuff." In an informal survey of books on divorce, the fate of the house itself and the financial assets were thoroughly covered, but the division of day-to-day possessions was ignored. One book, written for women, focused on how to manipulate the process to "get it all," but none addressed the emotional process of sorting out the physical effects of two merged lives.

One complication, of course, is that every relationship is different. Some divorces are mutual; others are hotly contested and brimming with bitterness. Even when there is agreement, the months around the split can be volcanic, spewing out all sorts of buried emotions and regrets. The decisions made at that time are not always sound.

The Rules of Breaking Up

Since there is so much variety in divorce, we have selected several real-life stories and extracted some principles from them. We hope you do not need the information—or need it again—but if you do, these may be helpful.

1. The party moving out does not forfeit all claim to the household goods, much less his or her personal belongings.

When Jon moved out of his home and in with Karin, whom he had been seeing secretly for almost a year, his main emotions were guilt toward his family and relief that the matter was finally resolved. Things were out in the open, and his life could move ahead. But it was a mistake, as he realized afterward, to believe that everything was settled. He had been so anxious to go that he had taken little but the clothes from his closet and his computer. He had also mistaken his wife, Linda's, acquiescence to liberal visitation for full cooperation.

Six months later, when Jon and his new love called it quits, he moved into an apartment and realized that he needed his stuff. When he approached Linda, she was happy to give him the old sofa from the family room—but little else. She stated that she needed the rest of the furniture to keep the house furnished for their children. To his shock, he found that she had sold or given away his books, his skis, and his old guitar. "You *left* them here," she pointed out. "I didn't think you wanted them."

Whether you feel that Linda was being disingenuous—if not spiteful—or that Jon got what he deserved, there are better ways to handle that kind of situation.

2. Don't give up your claim to the things you want or need and that are rightfully yours, just because it seems easier at the time.
People leave without their share of the possessions for other reasons as well, most notably when they are fleeing an abusive mate. Some feel that they have literally escaped with their lives. "I didn't want anything from that house," Becky shuddered. "It would only remind me of him." After 7 years of verbal abuse and belittling, her husband had begun to smash plates of food against the wall when he didn't like the meal and push her up against the wall during arguments; once he tried to choke her. Their small children were terrified.

Becky felt safe in the women's shelter and wanted to slam the door on her past life. She never wanted to see her husband again and was willing to forego everything from their home if she did not have to face his alternate begging and anger. But her counselor did not agree. Becky had every right to her childhood books, kitchenware, photographs, the children's toys, and the piano that *she* played; she was entitled to half the home's contents. When the case went to court for an Order of Protection, the judge set up a specific time for Becky to go to the home with a police escort and a U-Haul and take the things to which she was entitled.

3. Even when no one is forcing you, be as equitable as you can. It will save you regrets later on.

When Neil and Liz parted company, he moved into a small furnished home. The divorce was amicable, and he did not want most of the furniture. But when he asked for the curved-glass china cabinet they had bought when they were first married, Liz stalled. It was filled with dishes and glasses. After a while, she painted it light blue and moved it into her daughter's room to hold toys and stuffed animals. Many years later, it sits in her garage with one of the glass sides broken. "Every time I see it, I feel guilty," she said. "He wanted so few things. Why didn't I just *give* it to him?"

4. Despite what anybody says, take as much time as you need to get over the relationship.

After Rita was divorced, and the dust had settled, her practical mother came to visit. She did not approve of the fact that Rita still had pictures from her wedding on her dresser and souvenirs from their trips displayed in the living room. "You have to get on with your life," she scolded. "After all, *he* left *you*. It isn't healthy keeping all these reminders around—it isn't as if he'd died!"

A lot of people would agree with Rita's mother. Better to make a clean sweep, and get rid of any reminders, so you can start fresh—especially if, as in Rita's case, there are no children. But wait. While not advocating Miss Haversham as a role model—you may remember her as the *David Copperfield* character who kept the setup from her failed wedding day intact down to the decaying cake—we think that people need time to mourn. A divorce, after all, is the death of a relationship and needs to be processed the way any loss would.

Parents can also be allies in the process. When Ruth and her husband split up, Ron never came to the house again. Refusing to discuss anything with her, he insisted that all communication go through his lawyer's office. When her parents came to visit her, Ruth was stressed out and confused. Finally, her father said, "Why don't you girls go out to lunch? I'll take care of things here." While they were gone, he packed up all of Ron's clothes, tools, and sporting equipment, something Ruth had not been able to bring herself to do. She was forever grateful.

Even though she left a message for Ron through his attorney, he never claimed his things. After several months in the garage, they went to the Salvation Army. By then, she was happy to let them go.

5. Stay calm and think before you escalate the conflict by using physical belongings as a weapon.

By the time some couples get divorced, their actions and retaliations have become so tangled that no one can sort out what happened first. Lewis and Hannah's marriage, his second and her third, started off well, struggled at certain points, and ended in an explosion. Hannah sought a restraining order to keep him out of the house he had built, and they moved toward divorce. When things calmed down, he asked to be able to pick up some of his things, and she agreed, since she was going to be away for a few days.

Once in the house, Lewis found what he considered "evidence" that Hannah was seeing someone else, became furious, and left with most of the furniture as well as some of her personal items. From then on, Hannah could not relax until she had conducted a retaliatory raid on their weekend home. "His favorite thing is a painting of his grandchildren, and I'm taking it," she declared, and even her therapist could not dissuade her. Fortunately, the painting was not at the country house, but Hannah took enough other things to inspire Lewis to call and have the utilities in her home disconnected. She had to pay large deposits, with money she didn't have, to get the services restored in her name.

The momentary satisfaction of revenge can lead to consequences you will regret.

6. Take the opportunity to scale down to the life and belongings that truly represent *you*.

For people who married young and never had the experience of living alone, divorce can provide the first opportunity to scale down—and build up—to what they really love and what represents them. Although the discovery is broader than physical objects and covers all aspects of lifestyle and personality, the chance to re-create your physical environment is a gift.

Chances are, what you have is more about "us" than about you. Furniture was bought to fill space or because it was what a house "should" have, paintings were chosen to look good over the sofa, and so on. You have also matured in your tastes and interests and are no longer the youthful bride or groom. You'll find some ideas on how to proceed in Chapter 16, "Using Your Space for You."

9

MOVING IN A HURRY

"Help! We just had an open house for our home yesterday and received several offers. If we take the best, we have to be out in 2 weeks!"

Although you may have your new living situation already arranged, you never expected your old house to sell so quickly. And unless you have already been scaling down, you may be panicking right now.

Calm down.

Marj's sister, Wylla, found herself in this situation last year, and as agreed, Marj flew out to help her clear out her home. Driving home from the airport, Wylla said brightly, "You'll be proud of me. I already called the electric company and the phone company to have the service transferred."

"And?" Marj prodded.

"And?"

"Have you packed up much of your stuff?"

"No, nothing! I knew you were coming."

Marj sighed. It was going to be a busy 2 weeks.

BEFORE YOU LIFT A THING

Packing quickly doesn't mean packing in a rush. By taking care of these simple requirements in advance, you'll be able to work smarter and more easily.

The Right Stuff

Having the right supplies is not only helpful, it is a psychological necessity. Think of these as the Viagra of moving. And don't leave your home without them:

- Sturdy cartons with tops that close

- Clear packing tape and a tape gun

- Heavy plastic bags

- Colored markers

- A roll of clean newsprint paper or newspapers

- Large blank labels

- Multicolored dots

When you are working, keep these together in a recognizable container; it helps to avoid the repeated question, "Where is that marker *now?*"

Also consider buying a few of the clear plastic bins that are sold for storage; they are well priced at stores such as Target and can be used in the future to stow linens or holiday decorations. Now is not the time to rely on a ragtag collection of liquor store boxes and supermarket freebees. Go to a storage facility, home warehouse, or office supply store, and buy sturdy cartons.

For a price, some moving companies will pack up your home's contents for you; you may want to use professionals for china, glassware, and other fragile items. But they won't label what is in each carton or decide what goes and what should be discarded. In some situations, of course, there is simply no time for you to go through your belongings piece by piece. But understand that you will be paying to have items moved that you don't necessarily want in your new space and that you will have enough to do to get settled without the added work of scaling down then.

Say Cheese

Before you move a single piece of furniture, take some photographs. If you don't have a working camera, you can buy a disposable camera or two with a flash and 24 shots. Then photograph every room, from your cluttered basement to the study you love and the gardens outside. You will need to take several shots in the larger rooms to show everything. Do you *have* to do this? We think so. Although you can refer to the photos if you plan to recreate various rooms, they are even important to you if you don't. The photographs are a validation of the space in which you lived for a number of years, and having a visible reminder of them is important.

It is also the first step toward closure. If you start to get nostalgic or teary when you are taking pictures, that is fine. Even when you are anxious to move, leaving your current home is a bittersweet experience, and your emotions need to be expressed. You may think you will remember everything; perhaps you will. But having pictures of the inconvenient and annoying areas as well as the beautiful will keep you from overidealizing your old home in the future. Yes, the day lily garden was beautiful; but the cellar always smelled so damp.

Next, Create Zones

Although it sounds complicated, this is a simple procedure. Choose one place— a corner of the living room or the kitchen, for instance—that has room to sit down. Make this your stress-free zone. You and your helpers need a defined place to relax, have a cup of tea, and regroup when you feel overwhelmed. Knowing that you have a calm retreat helps keep the process under control. You will need to keep the area clear and have items you use frequently there: salt and sugar, light bulbs, paper towels, toilet paper, telephone directories—personal and yellow pages—reading glasses, a utility knife, and aspirin. On moving day, box these together, and keep them with you so that you know where they are in your new home.

The second key area is your giveaway zone. Pick an unused bedroom or back hallway for items and furniture that are neither going with you nor being trashed. These are items designated for "Family" or "Charity" and may include the belongings of your adult children as well. Put on a self-stick label, such as "Salvation Army" or "Susan," one that peels off easily as you make each decision. You may think you'll remember what you decided, but as items pile up, you probably won't. Furniture pieces that are too large to move can be labeled and left in place.

WHERE DO I START?

Where you begin packing up depends, in part, on how soon you have to move. If you are in a time crunch, start with the essential places in the house, and forget about the detached garage; you may be able to beg a little more time to get it cleared out if the new owners are able to move into the home itself. Even if you end up "renting" it from them for a month or two, it is better to be able to sort and dispense with a lot of what is stored there.

To prime the pump, select a room such as the dining room or guest bathroom, a place that is less complicated and not as emotionally exhausting. You need to remember that your focus has shifted from ordinary decluttering. There are three essential questions you should be asking about every piece you consider moving:

- Will it work in my new space?

- Is it worth the cost of moving it?

- Will my spirits rise when I unpack and see it?

The last question is the most important. This is your chance to have only what you *love* in your new space. Even if you have to go 2 months without a sofa while you look for one the color you've always wanted, in the long run, you'll wonder why you even considered hauling along the old wreck. You would have only had to discard it from your new place a short time later.

In one of our workshops, a woman raised her hand and shared her experience with moving. Because of her husband's employment, her family had to move into their new home before their old house was sold. Not wanting to appear desperate, they brought with them only what was essential and left their old house semi-furnished. When it sold 2 months later, they went back to clear it out. The only thing they brought back to their new house was a bread knife. "We were so thrilled to be living with only what we needed—life was so *easy*—that we didn't want our new home cluttered up with just stuff."

To Store or Not to Store?

At this point, you may be thinking, "What about storage?"

Storage can be a good idea. But only for a month or two and only if you have a firm plan.

THE MAIN QUESTION

Scaling down is different when you have to pack up in a hurry and move to another place. The question changes from "Is this still good?" to "Is this worth moving?"

Here are some typical items that should *not* make the move—a list to help you get started:

- *A near-empty bottle of hair conditioner or shaving lotion*
- *The rickety chair that everyone avoids sitting on*
- *A freestanding ironing board, when most of the time you spread a towel on the kitchen counter for a quick press*
- *An award-winning novel that puts you to sleep*
- *Holiday decorations you keep forgetting to use*
- *Cans of paint that are not the colors of your new place*
- *Address labels for your current home*
- *A bicycle roof rack when you no longer have working bicycles*
- *Curtains and drapes that do not fit your new windows*
- *A gift bottle of liqueur that was always too sweet for your taste*
- *Unread newspapers and magazines*
- *The carton in the basement that you never opened from your last move*

What are some good reasons to store furniture or other items temporarily? One is when you have a collection that is valuable, but which you are no longer interested in and don't have room for in your new space. You may want to sell the items on eBay or at a collector's convention. Since you know you will be disposing of the pieces as soon as you have time to make the arrangements and get a fair price, a temporary storage unit is better than a fire sale.

Another valid storage situation is when you need to finish up areas of your new space, such as refinishing the floors or finishing an upstairs area, and furniture would be a hindrance. Or you might temporarily store the belongings of an adult child who lives at a distance and cannot get home immediately, along with family items he would like to have. But have a definite plan for when he will be able to come. There is also the situation of the adult child or grandchild who wants some of the family furniture but "doesn't have room right now."

Two of Judi's organizing clients are struggling with this situation. Frank and Cecile's youngest daughter, Tammy, wanted the massive pedestal dining table, eight chairs, and matching china closet that they did not want to take to their new condo, but she was living in a studio apartment. The couple had bought the furniture second hand when they were first married, and though they did not have any particular attachment to it, they recognized that Tammy might. So they rented a storage unit, and because there was empty room left over, they added a few other pieces they did not want to make decisions about. Eight years later, they are still paying storage fees, and Tammy still does not have enough room for the furniture. As Frank says wryly, "We could have bought her several dining rooms by now."

Thinking in Color

Before you start packing, figure out your color coordination: blue for the living room, yellow for the kitchen, green for the dining room, etc. No, this isn't about decorating. You are going to choose a color for each room in your new place, and put that color dot on every carton or piece of furniture that goes in there. On moving day, put up a large color square at the entrance to each room so that the movers or your helpers will know where everything belongs. Even if the movers are only bringing your things inside the front door, the color system will help you to distribute boxes quickly.

So now you are standing in your Code Green dining room, anxious to get started. First, place several large green dots on all the pieces of furniture that are moving with you, including the rug. Next, pick out the china, glassware, and serving dishes that are definitely going; these are the pieces you will be happy to see again when you unpack. You can wrap groups of plates and bowls together in a stack with one layer between using bubble wrap or newsprint, rather than separately, if the walls of the box are well cushioned and the pieces are immobile inside. If it can't move, it won't break. If you are using newspaper, make sure you use two layers and scrunch (not fold) the top.

Wine glasses and tumblers have to be wrapped separately because of their shape—don't forget to cushion them with lots of scrunch—but trays, if pressed tightly against each other so they don't bounce or rub, can go as a group. Some people advocate wrapping breakables in bathroom towels or tablecloths since those have to be moved anyway. But we would rather see linens packed in neat stacks so they can be put away quickly where they belong. Picture all those crumpled linens in a heap on the floor, and then make your choice. On the other hand, they can be used to fill out boxes and still maintain their folds.

Once the carton is closed, write FRAGILE on the outside of the carton with a red marker and put on a green dot. There are two schools of thought on labeling cartons. One way is to number everything consecutively and, on a master sheet or in a notebook, list the number and describe in detail next to it what is inside the carton. That way, if you need to find something in your new place, you can refer to the notebook. The other way is to list on a blank label what is inside the carton. People who prefer this method point out that you are in trouble if you misplace the notebook or list and that it puts an end to "mystery cartons" that sit around unopened for years.

Special Helpers

What kept Marj and Wylla good-humored were Wylla's friends who participated in the process. A "foodie" helped out in the kitchen, spotting duplicates, and helping Wylla to be realistic about what she would need in her new condo. For her pains, she was given many of Wylla's 100-plus cookbooks. She was also happy to take jars and cans of exotic foods and ingredients that Wylla hadn't used yet.

A colleague from the university psychology department where Wylla had taught helped her sort through her study. She was happy to take materials that Wylla would no longer be using and was able to talk her out of saving outdated texts—"Wylla, this was published in 1962, and so much has happened in this field." More important, she also helped validate Wylla's long career by sharing memories and commenting on materials, such as "He really was a great writer, wasn't he? I still recommend this text!"

It was satisfying to Wylla to know that her things were going to eager homes. But there was also a psychological lifting of spirits to have other people around to help. Funny things seemed funnier and tragedies less devastating when they could be shared. When you can bring in younger relatives who are interested in family history, this is one last opportunity to tell stories about the items you're giving away.

If you are moving within the same area, take advantage of people's offers to help. They can transport hard-to-pack items such as lamps, plants, and computers, particularly if you have access to your new space before the actual move. You may not be able to get into your new home before moving day, of course. In that case, coordinate the traffic patterns so that "civilians" do not get in the way of professional movers. It helps to keep the items people will be bringing for you in a separate place, such as the garage or carport.

THE REMAINS OF THE DAY

Once you have packed the boxes of items that are going with you and described their contents, it is time to deal with the second group: items that are being given to specific organizations or individuals. Put the name label in a visible spot, and bring them to your giveaway zone. Will the dining room finally be empty? Not likely! There will always be a number of items that defy easy classification, things that you cannot picture going to a specific person or place, but hesitate to trash. You can't think of anyone who would like the cute boy and girl salt shakers you bought on a trip to Amish country or the cut glass ash tray since nobody smokes anymore.

Place these items in a separate section in your giveaway zone. They will be free for the taking by people who stop by to help or to pick up specific things you have put aside for them. But be discerning. Stubby candles, stained tablecloths, odd glasses and plates that are no longer part of a set, trays/candlesticks/salt shakers with the silver plate worn off, cracked bowls, and anything plastic should be headed for that large trash bag. Yes, *someone* would probably take them. But why encourage pack rat tendencies in other people or prolong the life of something whose usefulness has passed?

Interestingly, being discerning has an opposite side: Not everything that at first appears to be useless should be discarded. This was shown by the contents of Margaret's "sewing room." Although she had not made anything in years, there was still a pattern pinned to fabric, ready to be cut out. Stacks of material, boxes of thread, laces, trims, and vintage patterns were stored in the closet. At first glance, she was tempted to toss everything.

Fortunately, she didn't. Although home sewing was in decline for a while, it is undergoing a revival among people who are inspired by home decorating and craft demonstrations on TV. The fabrics and old patterns are often welcomed by theater companies to create vintage looks. In Margaret's case, a niece wanting to learn to sew took the 1970s machine that still worked, scissors, and thread. (The half-cut-out pattern was declined.)

When a room is finished, head for your stress-free zone to relax. You need to take breaks and even a nap if you can sleep during the day. Make meals a highlight, not a matter of grabbing a sandwich while you work or skipping food altogether. When you find you are getting overtired, *stop*. Signs of fatigue are a reluctance to make decisions, losing track of what you are doing, holding on to too much, or discarding more than you should. Most people have more energy in the morning and can tackle the physically or mentally difficult jobs then. Sit down to sort photos or papers in the afternoon.

The last thing to remember is to pack a suitcase as if you are going on a short trip. Include your next day's clothes, cosmetics, and medications. Having these handy makes you more ready to face the great task of unpacking.

One more thing: Remember that box of supplies in your stress-free zone? It will be equally important to have it at hand as you start to get settled. Besides the paper towels, spare lightbulbs, toilet paper, salt, sugar, aspirin, and a utility knife, you may want to add a flashlight, paper plates and plastic utensils, scissors, and your personal phone directory.

If you are moving any distance and have to tape the box up, write on the outside "Open Me First!"

part 4

SCALING DOWN
STRATEGIES

"There's more inside."

THE SAGA
OF THE RAIN BONNETS

One reason that we've been successful in helping people organize and scale down is that we have varied our techniques to fit their specific personalities. In this chapter, we will explore which methods might suit you best.

Remember rain bonnets? They were those clear plastic squares that fanned open to cover your hair, then snapped back together when you tugged on the ends. Once closed, they could be stored in a very small space. The downside was that they tied under your chin and looked silly. They may have been sold in some pharmacies, but most of the time, they were given away by businesses, with their name in gold letters on the plastic case.

GROUPING

When Judi was helping an older client, Anna, get ready to move, rain bonnets began popping up like toadstools after rain. After the fifth or sixth had surfaced, Judi gestured at the pile and said, "Looks as though you've got enough to keep you dry."

But Anna shook her head. "I like to take extras with me when we go on vacation. That way I can hand them out to people who need them."

Okay. When number 13 sprang from a kitchen drawer, Judi said, "You've got more than enough to give away."

But Anna shook her head again. "I have to see how many I have before I get rid of any of them. When I get them all in one pile, I'll decide."

In its way, it made sense. For people who have so many duplicates that they can't remember what they own, the only way to feel sure they have kept the best is by seeing them all together first. Even rain bonnets. Grouping is one way to know exactly what you are keeping before you give anything away.

So group if you have to, but keep only as many as you need.

SKIMMING

The opposite technique of grouping is skimming. We call it that in homage to the old-fashioned milk bottles that were delivered with the cream on top. The bottle would be shaken, the cream distributed evenly through the rest of the milk, if a greedy child had not gotten to it first and dipped her fingers in. Skimming here refers to keeping the best, the cream, and giving everything else away without worrying about it.

At the end of this chapter, there is a list of the most common items you would use in your home, with a space to indicate how many you feel you need to own. If, next to "___ sets of dishes," you write in "2," one for company and one to use every day, you would then choose your two favorites. Any others, including "orphans" from sets that no longer exist, would automatically be given away without further thought. It can help to have someone else—a spouse or good friend or organizer—remove and recycle the others for you.

Skimming Complications

If you can stick to this resolve, skimming works well with everything from winter coats to serving trays. It eliminates a lot of decision making and second guessing and takes away the temptation to create exceptions for certain items. But you may find that it works well for you in some categories and not in others. For instance, you go to your coat closet with every intention of skimming off one good winter coat, one warm jacket, one raincoat, and one ski parka. That will give you something warm to wear for every occasion.

But then you see the other outerwear, perfectly good in its way, and are assailed by "What ifs?" "What if my winter jacket is at the cleaners, and it snows?" "What if I'm invited to the White House for a week, and they see me wearing the same old coat every day?" (If you're invited to the White House for a week, it won't be because of your wardrobe.) But memories and insecurities can sabotage you as they did Rachel, one of our first workshop participants.

Under the Surface

When Rachel began scaling down her family's belongings, she made real progress until she got to their coats, jackets, down vests, and other outerwear. Looking into the jammed closet and imagining herself removing half the items to give to charity, she started to become anxious. Finally, she left the closet and moved on to the leftover cans of paint in the garage.

Telling her husband about her reaction that night, she suddenly had an image of a man in a patched and shabby overcoat selling apples on a street corner during the Great Depression. He was shivering as the wind whipped around a corner, and people passed him by. Rachel's parents had come of age during the 1930s, and although they had not been as personally affected as many people had by the Depression, they still had many stories of hard times.

It did not take Rachel long to realize what she had been thinking: "What if there's another Depression? What if we lose our jobs, or they are unable to pay us? What if we run out of warm clothes and have no money to buy more?"

Once she understood the fears that she hadn't realized were there and made peace with them, she was able to pare down the family's outerwear with no problem. While she was not able to skim in that area, there were others in which she was more successful.

Conquering the "What Ifs?"

To return to the example of skimming off two sets of dishes and giving away the rest, you may start to do so, then be tripped up by a thought as simple as "What if I want to give a buffet dinner for 50 people and use real china?"

If you stop at that point, you'll find yourself with an excuse to hold on to everything. You need to ask yourself some other questions: How often do I actually entertain that way? Can I just as easily rent 50 white plates from a party supply shop, along with wine glasses, chairs, and chafing dishes? Do people actually prefer balancing heavier china plates on their laps while holding a glass as well? Is it a matter of graciousness or a matter of wanting to seem like the perfect host/hostess, perfectly equipped for every occasion?

In other words, when you are scaling down and objections come up, don't accept them at face value. Go deeper, and find out what your feelings are based on.

PERFORMING TRIAGE

We talk about using triage in our chapter on collections, but the process can be applied in many different ways. Books, costume jewelry, neckties, and coffee mugs all lend themselves to this process. Ah, those coffee mugs! In the 1970s, technology made it easy to transfer an image onto a shiny ceramic surface, and an industry bloomed. Most homes still have an assortment that includes at least one of the following: a floral motif with "World's Best Mom," a black "Over the Hill" birthday mug, a souvenir of Disney World, a reproduction of Van Gogh's "Sunflowers," a bonus mug with a public radio or TV logo, whimsical animals with French names, such as Le Chat, a "Far Side" cartoon, and a sports theme.

We don't drink out of all of them, of course. We tend to use the same two or three over and over: the ones that feel good in our hand or hold just the right amount of coffee or tea. If you have mugs jostling for space (or ties, handbags, CDs, etc.), it is time to perform an exorcism by triage. Gather all your items in one place. Then set the first three apart, and put the one you care about least off to the side, separating it from the two others. Then select another group of three, and do the same. By the end of your sorting, you will have eliminated the one-third you like least and kept your favorites. If you are moving to a smaller space, consider eliminating one out of two.

Can you stack the deck? Absolutely. There is nothing wrong with putting one you don't like in the group of three. You'll still end up with the same result.

TAKE A PHOTOGRAPH

Can a picture take the place of an actual thing? You'd be surprised. If you have a photograph of you in your wedding dress or of a speedboat you had some years earlier, or of the crib quilt you made for your daughter when she was born, it doesn't matter if you still physically have possession of these things. You can look at the pictures and remember the experience or item and show it to other people. If you've created a beautiful garden and are moving, photograph it from various vantage points before you go. You'll get a lot of satisfaction from being able to look at pictures of what you created.

The same is true for various areas in your current home. You may have no desire to replicate them in your new space, but it is satisfying to have a record for yourself. And if you are creating a new space where you live, be sure to take a roll of "Before" and "After" photos.

"I Was Wearing That When . . ."

Taking a photograph also works well for clothing. Men may become attached to certain items, usually quite worn, in which they feel comfortable. Women tend to become sentimental about specific outfits in their closet. A small, charming book by Ilene Beckerman, *Love, Loss, and What I Wore* has drawings of the clothing she was wearing at momentous occasions, beginning with childhood and moving through marriage, divorce, deaths, and celebrations. As women, we have traditionally had more opportunity for variety and have given more thought to the effect of what we wear.

There is an entire chapter on our relationship to clothing, "The Secret Life of Clothing," but we mention clothes here because they are prime candidates as photographic subjects. Rather than keeping outfits that you know you will never wear again, think about making your own version of "What I Wore." You can start by scanning and printing or color copying older photographs in which you were wearing a favorite outfit, then take some pictures of favorite clothing you want to get rid of now. You will be surprised at how easy it becomes to let the physical item go.

SHRINK IT

How do you make something smaller? One way is by stripping it down to its essentials. That means getting rid of outer envelopes, entire magazines or journals, cookbooks from which you only use one or two recipes. Save the letters or cards, remove the specific article you need, photocopy the recipes, and give the book away. Purge those empty cartons you're saving in case you need to return something; in the unlikely event that an appliance needs to go back for repairs, you can have a professional company such as Mailboxes Etc. box it up for you.

If you have a tattered family quilt, make a pillow from an area of it that is still intact or have one made for you. The still-good parts of a handmade lace tablecloth that has gotten stained in places makes a pretty window valence. Combine a lot of little photographs into a larger frame with a collage mat or attractive wrapping paper background. If you don't want to haul around a stack of heavy yearbooks, consider removing the pictures and parts pertinent to you and framing them or adding them to your Life Book (see Chapter 12), discarding the annuals themselves.

HOW MANY _____ DO YOU NEED?

The beauty of the following list is that it works equally well for people setting up a home or apartment for the first time, those merging two households through marriage, and people who are scaling down or getting ready to move. The list is designed to help you stick to your resolve. Go over it, and fill in the amounts as if you are doing it for someone who wants to live a streamlined life. Feel free to put a zero next to anything that does not seem necessary to you.

We'll let you in on a secret. In cookbooks, woodworking and craft manuals, books on makeup, home decorating guides, and the like, there is always a list of tools and materials you will need. The list for setting up a well-equipped kitchen, for instance, can run to several pages. A guide to wallpapering will have nine or 10 items without which you cannot complete the project—and then will own forever.

The secret, based on personal experience, is that you can get by happily with far fewer items. While it may be fun to have a copper omelet pan or electric screwdriver or a pizza wheel, you can make eggs or hang shelves or slice a pie very easily without them. You will also have three less things to store and care for. Before you thoroughly outfit yourself at a craft store, consider the beauty of the cave paintings at Lascaux or the stained glass windows in Chartres Cathedral and the very rudimentary tools that produced them. In other words, there may be some items on the following list that you have no need for and others that you need to add.

Home Inventory

We have deliberately jumbled the items so that you consider each individually, and your eyes do not glaze over from spending too long in one room. As suggested, it is helpful to pretend to select the number of items for someone else, someone who wants to live a fulfilling but streamlined life or is setting up a home for the first time. If you find your concentration flagging, stop and finish later.

Put the number of items you feel a home needs beside each object.

____ *Coffee mugs*

____ *Muffin tins*

____ *Wine bottle openers*

____ *Drills*

____ *Sets of dishes*

____ *Videos*

____ *Bathroom towels*

____ *Coffee makers*
(espresso, cappuccino, infusion, automatic drip, urn style)

____ *Phones and answering machines*

____ *Measuring cups*

____ *Gym bags*

____ *Everyday drinking glasses*

____ *Screwdrivers*

____ *Toothbrushes*

____ *Food storage containers (glass and plastic)* •

____ *Vacuum cleaners*

____ *Cake and pie tins*

____ *Candlesticks*

____ *TV sets*

____ *Frying pans*

____ *Pancake turners*

____ *Lawn mowers*

____ *Measuring spoons*

____ *Hair dryers*

____ *Old prescriptions and medications*

____ *Lesser-used gadgets (egg slicers, pizza wheels, apple corers, melon ballers, ice cream scoops, candy thermometers, etc.)*

____ *CDs*

____ *Blankets*

____ *Bottles of aspirin*

____ *Decorative pillows*

____ *Knives (bread, carving, paring)*

____ *Baskets*

____ *Cleaning rags*

____ *Rakes*

____ *Potato peelers*

____ *Plastic bags*

____ *Briefcases*

____ *Platters and trays*

____ *Paper grocery bags*

____ *Books*

____ *Electric shavers*

____ *Specialty cookware (crepe pan, slow cooker, wok, omelet pan, deep fryer, fondue pot)*

____ *Trivets and hot tiles*

____ *Fireplace tools*

____ *DVD players*

____ *Flatware, silverware*

____ *Hammers*

____ *Shopping bags*

____ *Bar glasses (all kinds)*

____ *Framed pictures with no place to hang them*

____ *VCRs*

____ *Suitcases*

____ *Wine glasses*

____ *Make-up (the wrong colors, gift packs, eyelash curlers)*

____ *Flower vases*

____ *Coasters*

____ *Shower curtains*

____ *CD players*

____ *Candles (all kinds)*

____ *Clocks (wall and travel)*

____ *Tablecloths and cloth napkins*

____ *Appetizer serving dishes*

____ *Tape decks and Walkmans*

____ *Curlers, hot rollers, curling iron*

____ *Cleaning supplies*

____ *Comforters*

____ *Empty photo albums*

____ *Computers*

____ *Whisks*

____ *Foreign language instruction tapes*

____ *Tennis rackets*

____ *Holiday decorations*

____ *Cameras*

____ *Spare tires*

____ *Saws*

____ *Catalogs*

____ *Kitchen timers*

____ *Coat racks*

____ *Lawn ornaments*

____ *Musical instruments*

When you have finished selecting the ideal number of items for another person, go through and add up the number of items. There may not seem to be that many individually, but remember that each of them will take up a physical space, and they are in addition to furniture, clothing, jewelry, foodstuffs, mail, and the daily newspaper.

When you are feeling strong, compare the number of items you selected as "necessary" to the number of the ones that you actually have. If your own numbers are larger, don't panic. Just keep the list as a goal to attain. If your numbers are smaller, you can go to the head of the class!

FINDING GOOD HOMES

When Judi's neighbor Jeff realized it was time to get another car, he was still attached to his 8-year-old van. It had hauled a myriad of things home, from Christmas trees to wing chairs, and had taken him across the country at least once. The van started up without fail even on frigid mornings. But it no longer felt as safe as it once had, especially on winter roads. He wanted to donate the van to a charity where it would actually be used and not end up being sold by the organization as scrap.

There were many willing charities listed in the local paper in the automotive classified section and also online, found by typing in "Automobile Donation." After looking into a local organization, he found that it had a spotty reputation, with no one able to figure out who it actually benefited. Next, he called the local office of a national charity he knew was reputable and did the kind of work he supported. The person he spoke to was enthusiastic and gave him another number to call. He left a message, but no one called back.

Finally, another neighbor told him about a nearby church that accepted donations of cars for needy families in the community. He talked to them, found it was true, and felt satisfied when they came to get the van and gave him a tax receipt.

Knowing that the belongings you are not keeping are going to be appreciated is important. Few of us want to think we are contributing one more thing to the landfill if there is any way to prevent it. It takes time and a little ingenuity to find the best home for certain items, but there is an increased sense of accomplishment when you do.

DISPOSAL OPTIONS

You have basically four choices for finding new places for things you no longer need:

- Give them to family and friends

- Sell them through various venues

- Donate them to a charitable organization

- Recycle/trash them appropriately

When you are dramatically downsizing or clearing out an older relative's home, you will probably utilize all of these, so we'll cover each option in detail. But how to choose what is best to do?

When Judi and her brothers realized it was time to sell their parents' home (Dad was gone and Mom permanently in assisted living), they were faced with a huge task. Their parents had become devotees of estate auctions in their golden years, an interest that exacerbated Dad's pack rat tendencies and enlarged Mom's collection of bisque dolls and marble-topped tables. Neither could resist a bargain, so the large basement held many lame ducks and curiosities. Dad had also filled up a storage shed on the property and rented another one from a friend.

The situation was more complicated because two of the three siblings lived out of town.

Judi began sorting through the papers, which she could haul home with her, and her brothers cleared out the storage shed (the friend was selling his property). Next, they rented the largest available dumpster for the weekend. With their spouses and children, they filled the walk-in container with debris from the garage and half of the basement, putting anything still usable beside the curb, where it was snatched up immediately by passing drivers. One man with a flatbed truck was so friendly that they began bringing out items to offer him.

Making Choices

It took time to prepare emotionally for the next step: taking what they wanted for themselves. They chose a Friday morning, first assuring each other that what was important was their relationship as brothers and sister and that the things in the house were, ultimately, *things.* They also realized that their parents, who had valued family harmony, would have been devastated if there were disagreements or fighting over their belongings. Only Judi and her brothers were present and used a system of taking turns to choose. That way, the more valuable items such as rugs or lamps could be evenly divided.

As expected, Judi took the fewest things physically, choosing only items for which she had a place. She was also the family "historian," having salvaged photos and older papers from her sorting out.

At the end of the morning, the three of them felt satisfied with what they had of their parents' belongings and felt uplifted by having done it together. Being in the house had evoked memories and funny stories, fond recollections of the family they had been, an opportunity to feel the sadness that those times were permanently gone. Although there had been some knockdown, drag-out family fights in the past, by keeping focused, they were able to work harmoniously in their old home.

And then at noon, as previously arranged, an auction company came and packed up whatever they felt they could successfully sell. In turn, the company recommended a dealer who would come in and literally take everything else away at no charge. That person would make a profit on the salable items left and would dispose of what was broken or unappealing. The money from the auction went into Judi's mother's account, going toward her care and benefiting the causes she and Judi's father had supported.

Although every story will be different, there are similarities when it comes to finding good homes. We will cover all the possibilities in this chapter, from the beautiful Welsh cupboard you no longer have room for, down to the stack of "vintage" tires you aren't sure what to do with.

GIVING TO FAMILY AND FRIENDS

In earlier times, it was popular to specify in a will exactly who would receive which treasures. That custom made for high drama, at least in films, with family and servants gathered in an office as a lawyer intoned, "And to my cook, Mary Ames, for her years of devotion, I bequeath my . . ." There would always be an upsetting bequest—or lack of one—and a family member would storm out of the room.

But with more and more people scaling down and moving to smaller spaces, another pattern is emerging. People are feeling a need to divest themselves *now*, and it has become common to pass on family keepsakes to children and other relatives and have the pleasure of seeing their reactions. People are also finding out ahead of time who is interested in having which items. And this can create some drama of its own.

What do you do, for instance, if you have a son who lives in a studio apartment and has no interest in "stuff" and a daughter in a large Victorian home who values and wants everything you have? Throw in a daughter-in-law divorced from another son, but who wants to make sure *her* children get their fair share of their grandparents' belongings, and you have the ingredients for high drama indeed.

High drama, especially when you realize that there is no magic formula for distribution. You cannot force your nonmaterialistic son to accept his grandparents' curio cabinet, and you see no point in dividing up silverware so that everyone has two or three place settings, but no one has enough with which to entertain. Alternatively, you are not sure if it is fair to penalize younger family members who want to maintain the family heritage and possessions by leaving them less "titled property" (real estate, stocks and bonds, bank accounts, automobiles, interest in a business) in your will. But rather than doing nothing, it is better to choose one of the following alternatives:

See what they think is fair. Discuss the situation with other family members, and find out what seems equitable to them. They may not be in total agreement, and you may be surprised at how they feel. But it will help you make a decision they can live with amicably. When you have decided, let them know the details.

Your family will be able to accept it better hearing it from you rather than getting an unpleasant surprise when you are gone.

Let them choose now. Ask your children and grandchildren privately to pick out several things in your home of which they are fond and would like to have. Then, when you are ready to part with those items, start giving them as birthday or Christmas/Hanukkah gifts. That way, you can see their pleasure and also tell them any stories or memories connected with the gift—how it came to be in the family and what it means to you. A secondary gain is that you don't have to spend as much time shopping!

If they are interested in things that you plan to continue using, create a list, and append it to your will. Your lawyer or executor can tell you the exact procedure because it varies from state to state.

GIVING TO OTHER PEOPLE

Sometimes, we make the mistake of assuming that everything we own has to be passed down to our children. But this attitude ignores a whole other group—our friends, other relatives, and the organizations to which we belong. If you know that a sterling silver tea set would collect more dust than use in a child's home, donate it to your church women's group or another organization to which you belong that holds receptions. If a young neighbor has always admired a painting of yours, give it to him. Collections with historic value can go to museums.

Fear

The chapter "Clearing Out Your Family Home" discusses personal dynamics in more detail, but one pitfall to mention here is the cautionary tale of the Boston heiress, Isabella Gardner (see box). This is based on the fear that your cherished possessions won't get the proper respect or care. When Marj was helping an older couple scale down to move to a condo, Lily told her, "I know my daughter Alison wants my dishes. She's loved that china since she was a little girl; Jon and I bought it on our honeymoon in New York. But Ali is *not* a great housekeeper, and she has all those children! I'm afraid it's just going to get broken."

Marj didn't say anything at that time, and they went on working. But later on, she asked Lily gently, "What's the most important thing to you about the china?

Is it that it be forever preserved, even if it's by someone outside the family? Or is it that Alison, who loves the dishes, has them to use?"

Lily understood immediately. "Of course, it's not the dishes. They're just *things*; once I give them up, I can't control what happens to them. And I don't want to! Ali is my dear daughter, and her pleasure in them is what's really important."

You may have to make this mental adjustment with certain of your own belongings, particularly collections. Judi's mother hoped that her large antique doll collection would be kept intact. Although it was not really suitable to be donated to a museum, she had spent years amassing the bisque dolls and was attached to them. But none of her children had the space or the desire to have a separate "doll room," and some dolls eventually found their way to other, eager homes.

SELLING

In the past 10 years, there have been great changes in this area; traditional antique dealers have been caught between the new opportunities people have to sell over the Internet and some inflated expectations raised by programs such as the *Antiques Roadshow*. Dealers still advertise to buy your silver, china, furniture, or "collectibles"; used-book shop owners will still pay you to cart your library away; but

---

"THE ISABELLA GARDNER SYNDROME"

Isabella Stewart Gardner, a New York City heiress, began buying Titians, Botticellis, Rembrandts, and other works of art in Europe to relieve her depression after the death of her young child. She and her husband settled in Boston, where she established a collection that she bequeathed to the city with the stipulation that if so much as a candlestick were moved, everything was to be sold in Paris, and the money given to Harvard University.

Needless to say, everything in the Isabella Stewart Gardner Museum has remained unchanged, even to the blank space on the wall where a Vermeer painting hung before it was stolen. In her final years, she would sometimes rear up in her bed and cry out, "You there! Don't touch!" to imaginary strangers. Her ghost is said to return to the museum once a month to make sure everything is exactly as she left it.

as a seller, you have many more options. There are online auctions such as eBay, reliable consignment shops, tag or garage sales with professionals doing the work for you. If you want to do it yourself, many local papers will give you signs to post and a list of suggestions.

Antique Dealers

If time is an issue, and you decide you want to sell your valuables outright, consult the yellow pages under "Antiques" or "Collectibles" or "Book Dealers—Used" for an established firm or shop. The reason to look for a *reputable* dealer is that they are bound by law to offer you a fair price. It is illegal for them to take a look at your Sheraton sideboard and give you $15. Because they are presumed to have expert knowledge, and you aren't, they are not allowed to take advantage of you. As well as using the yellow pages, ask other people in your community for recommendations. After you make an appointment, an antique or book dealer will come to your home, look at what you are interested in selling, and offer you a price. Occasionally you may, like the owners of family heirlooms on the *Antiques Roadshow,* be happily surprised. But most of the time, you'll simply feel that the price is fair or even feel some letdown that your belongings aren't worth more. You'll need to remember that the dealer has a good idea of what your items will sell for and has to pay for advertising, running a shop, and other expenses. Although you paid $28.95 for that bestseller 3 years ago, if there are 100,000 copies in print, the book may have little resale value.

It is the responsibility of the dealer to remove the purchased items at no cost to you.

Going, Going, Gone!

Auction houses work differently. They will try to make a phone assessment as to whether your items would be appropriate for their venue. If they are, a representative will come to your home and arrange for the items to be brought to their showroom. Some auction houses will take everything or even arrange to hold the sale at your home. Others will select only what they want. Although they charge a commission of around 30 percent, they will work hard to get the best possible price for you (and themselves) and usually have a buying clientele they can rely on. It will probably be several months before your items are scheduled to be sold.

You will be sent a list, usually with estimates of how much a specific piece is expected to bring. There is also a price, not listed, below which the auctioneer will not accept bids. Besides the people who attend the auction in person, most houses accept sealed bids from buyers who cannot be there and will telephone interested parties who want to bid on a particular item. This is all to your advantage.

Should you attend the sale yourself? It depends on how emotionally invested you are in your things, how open you are to hearing other people's positive—and negative—comments about them. There is no practical reason for you to attend; trust your gut feeling on this decision.

Within 30 days of the auction, you will receive an accounting that lists every item sold and the price it brought, and a check for that amount minus their commission and, in many cases, minus a fee for transporting your goods to the sale. Ask the representative about any additional charges beside their commission, so that you will not be unpleasantly surprised.

The Professional Tag Sale

Another option, if you are not interested in selling your things yourself, is to have a tag sale handled by professionals. These people, who advertise in the "Merchandise" or "Tag Sale" section of the newspaper classified ads, will come to your home, evaluate and price what you have, and arrange advertising, then on the day of the sale, they will handle everything. Some will even sell automobiles. Most of the time, they charge a commission of 25 to 30 percent, a percentage of the sales, but one antique dealer we know will do it for the opportunity of having first crack at what you are selling. It has become harder and harder for dealers to find good merchandise. If they are planning to purchase some pieces themselves, try to ascertain that what they are offering you is a fair price.

If you have time, look in the classified ads for several sales run by professionals, then stop by. This will give you a good feel for what type of merchandise they do handle best and how they run the sale. Talk to the ones you are impressed with about doing a sale for you, and ask if you can speak with the homeowners afterward to get their recommendation.

Do It Yourself

Professionals depend, of course, on your having enough valuable items or mem-orabilia to make it worth their while and to uphold their reputation for running quality sales. You might decide to have your own sale or do one with a friend or neighbor if you have a lot of miscellaneous goods or furniture that you know you will not bring top dollar. These things include everyday dishes and baking pans, household appliances, lawn furniture and gardening supplies, baby items, records, kitchen table sets, knickknacks, framed pictures, fans, and so on. We've been to sales where people have lined up to buy half-used cans of Freon from the garage—virtually anything is salable, as long as the price is right!

Most of us are familiar with yard sales. Too familiar. But if you haven't been to any recently, we suggest you go (for research purposes), paying attention to effec-tive signs (large enough to be easily read from a car), the layout of items for sale, prices, handling of money, and general atmosphere. Notice what is a turnoff, such

---

WHY HAVE A PROFESSIONAL RUN YOUR TAG SALE?

Why should you pay a commission to someone else for something that looks so easy? You just run a few ads, put prices on stuff, and take in the money. Right? Wrong—at least according to a number of tag sale dealers to whom we asked the question. Here is what they said:

- *We know the present market value of every item in the household. We are able to identify "valuable treasures" that the homeowner doesn't know about.*
- *We make it a lot easier and less stressful for our customers, especially if they are moving.*
- *We have a book filled with buyers looking for certain items.*
- *It saves people time and energy.*
- *With our expertise, we get the best prices for all merchandise.*
- *We know how to organize, arrange, advertise, and, most important, how to sell!*
- *I take the time to polish silver, clean furniture, and wash and shine crystal and china.*
- *My sales are known for their quality, and I get excellent prices.*

as things that are ridiculously expensive (making you doubt all the pricing), large items without a price tag, and sellers who act as if you are trying to cheat them.

PLANNING A SALE

Professional sellers have no shortage of advice for you in organizing and running your garage sale.

Pay attention to timing. Make sure you aren't planning your sale for a major holiday weekend when people will be involved in celebrations. If you live in an area that attracts tourists, schedule your sale between July and September, and post a lot of signs downtown.

Do it in a day. Unless you have a large quantity of stuff, you'll have better luck with a 1-day sale, preferably on a Saturday. Most second days of a 2-day sale aren't worth your while because buyers believe things are already picked over and stay away.

Advertise, advertise, advertise. Since garage sale mavens go through the ads and plot out a route in advance, putting an ad in several local papers along with a brief description of what you have is important. Phrases such as "40 years' accumulation" are magical.

Use curb appeal. Put a handful of balloons outside your house; it's festive and makes people slow down automatically to see what's going on. Arrange several of your most appealing items out front, encouraging passersby to stop. And make things look as attractive and well-cared-for as you can; wrinkled clothing draped over a car does not set the best tone.

Price low. People are not expecting to pay antique store prices. And they won't. One rule of thumb is to ask yourself how much *you* would pay for a particular item, and price it accordingly. Buyers will always ask, "Can you do better on this?" so keep that in mind. That way, if you can offer people something off the marked price, everyone feels satisfied. An alternative is to put your lowest figure and post a sign saying, "Prices are firm," but that isn't really part of the game.

Cash flow. Price items in 25-cent increments, so you won't have to worry about stocking nickels and dimes for change. Speaking of change, get more $1 and $5 bills from the bank than you think you'll ever need. Especially first thing in the morning, everyone will want to pay with a $20 bill from the cash machine.

If you have fewer than four sales a year, you aren't responsible in most states for collecting sales tax.

Remains of the day. If your sale is winding down with items still unsold, accept any offer—especially for bulky items. You will probably be putting them out by the curb for free or donating them to some charity. Don't overpersonalize your leftovers. If no one wanted your gold-painted garden Buddha, don't feel rejected on his behalf.

Enjoy the results. And why not? You'll have more money and less stuff.

A Cautionary Word

If you have mixed feelings about having to sell your things or those of family members, don't do it yourself. When Paul and Ginger, two newly retired teachers, found a collection of Majolica plates they wanted at a Long Island yard sale, they declined to buy one with a hairline crack. The homeowner flew into a rage. She accused them of questioning her integrity and refused to sell them *any*. When she saw that they had purchased several art books from a table outside and learned what they had paid for them, she started screaming that they were stealing from her. Obviously, her circumstances for having to sell weren't happy ones and were perhaps exacerbated by the sight of a carefree couple her own age.

If you can handle a sale, however, and are happy to see your things going to good homes, it can be fun and profitable.

Online Auctions

When eBay first opened as a sales venue, uploading photographs and information was a challenge best left to the computer literate. But every year, as technology improved, it became easier; now much of the work is done for you. If you still feel hesitant, eBay will recommend someone who lives near you who can take your items, photograph and list them, then mail the sold item out, for a percentage of the price realized.

At the current time, there are well over a million items for sale on eBay every hour. Even if you are not interested in auctioning anything off, it is a valuable guide to what a particular item is worth—"worth" being, of course, what someone somewhere will pay for it. To find out what something is currently selling for, use the Internet to go to eBay, click on "Search" in the menu bar, and on that page, type in several words about the item. Scroll down the page to the link "More Search Options" and click it. That will take you to a screen where you can select "Completed items only."

Although eBay will prompt you through the forms and process, for more specific hints, see "How to Sell on eBay" (page 152).

DONATING

The most satisfying thing about donating still-useful items is that they will live on and be appreciated by someone else. In many cases, they will increase a family's or individual's quality of life. The following list shows how to find good homes by category:

Books and Videos

People are often in a quandary about where to donate their libraries. There are books and there are *books*. Not every volume is worth saving. You can toss paperbacks in poor condition—browned pages, loose binding, print too small to read—and all books that have old information about medicine, census statistics, science, or health. Add to the pile *Reader's Digest* condensed books and old textbooks. Photography and computer manuals and travel guides become outdated very quickly. Older classics in cheap bindings can go as well.

Once you have applied these criteria, look for homes for the books that are left in the following places:

Library and nonprofit book sales. Even if your library does not accept donations for sales or for their own collection, many do. You can find out by asking around or going to an Internet site called "Book Sales in America." By clicking on your state and narrowing it down further, you can locate both ongoing shops and one-time book sales. Most sales now include videos and CDs.

Day-care centers and schools. Children's books can be expensive to buy and are not always included in the budget, so if you have some that are in good condition, most day-care or elementary school teachers will be delighted. Children are hard on books, especially on those they love, so a fresh supply is always appreciated. One couple we know makes a point of buying kids' books at the sales they go to, cleaning them up if necessary, and donating them in their community.

Senior centers and assisted living facilities. Before you bring them books, ask if there are specific types they want. Some may only need large print or light fiction. Other elder communities have impressively organized libraries and welcome a wide variety of subjects. Veterans' homes seem especially interested in tapes, videos, and CDs.

National organizations. If you live in St. Paul, Minnesota, or Washington, D.C., or don't mind shipping books (for best rates use fourth class, media mail) these two organizations will accept your donations:

HOW TO SELL ON EBAY

While selling online has become easier every year, it can still seem intimidating at first. You will need to set up an account, which means your personal information and a credit card from which they can deduct any commissions. You will choose a user name and a password, which you can use for buying or selling.

The following are hints from some experienced eBay sellers:

Do your research. Look up the item on eBay before you begin to see how many are currently for sale and what price they are bringing. If there seems to be a glut of items that aren't getting decent selling prices, don't bother listing yours.

Use photos. Take pictures of the item from several angles. Either use a digital camera, or simply use a regular film camera, reserve the roll for eBay items, and have it developed onto a CD instead of as prints. Name and crop the prints, and leave them on your computer desktop. For a small charge, eBay will retrieve them and store the images on their site.

Know which options to select. It is worthwhile to pay the fee, usually 25 cents, to have a thumbnail picture next to your listing, but don't bother with gift icons.

Write your heading carefully. The number of characters you are allowed to use is limited, so put dates and other facts as keywords, not empty descriptives such as "pretty" or "unique." These will be words that buyers will use to search and find your item.

Books for Africa (www.booksforafrica.org) is happy to accept textbooks from elementary school through college, except for foreign language and American history. The books should be in new or barely used condition, 10 years old or newer, and they are especially interested in children's and young adults' hardcover storybooks, science and math books, and dictionaries. Encyclopedias should be the current edition and *National Geographic* magazines from 1985 on are also acceptable. Send to Books for Africa, 253 E. 4th Street, St. Paul, MN 55101.

Books for America (www.booksforamerica.org) is looking for reading that would be suitable for shelters, prisons, hospices, and community organizations as well as videos and DVDs. Their top priority, however, is children's books in good condition. They do *not* want textbooks. Books can be mailed to Books for America, 2800 Quebec Street NW, Suite 744, Washington, D.C. 20008.

Choose a good time to close your auction. Because people often bid at the last minute, it makes sense to pick out an evening hour, preferably on a weekend, instead of letting your auction end at 3 o'clock in the morning.

Don't start your opening bid too high. Naturally, you're nervous about getting the price you want, but even though they will work their way up to it, in the beginning, bidders like to think that they're going to get a bargain. You can also set a hidden reserve price, meaning that if the highest bid doesn't meet this price, the item will not sell.

Calculate postage beforehand. That way, you can include the amount in your information. If you are uncertain about mailing costs, take the item to your local post office or UPS center, and ask. You can also calculate the approximate amount over the Internet at the USPS and UPS sites.

Be philosophical about the results. It's a good idea to begin with items you are willing to let go of easily. Sometimes you will be amazed at how much an old auto manual brings. Other times something that should sell well doesn't. Expect this and realize that it will even out over time.

Have fun! The best reason for auctioning things on eBay is enjoyment. It's fun to watch the prices rise and see what happens with the bidding in the last few minutes. You'll be tempted at first to check every couple of hours for changes. If you don't get a kick out of the process, you'll probably find it too much work.

Clothing

The most popular places for donating clothing are charities such as the Salvation Army, Goodwill Industries, Vietnam Veterans of America, etc., which have retail stores. If your clothing is in nice condition, beware of the large bins (usually pink) that are located in shopping centers and other central locations. They collect clothing for charities such as PAL, which are legitimate, but the clothing generally gets bundled up and sold by the pound to be recycled.

If some of the clothing has been in your closet long enough to be considered "vintage," consider passing it on to high school or college drama departments or little theater groups. Hats, purses, and other accessories are wonderful for this purpose. Most plays have some kind of period setting, if only the recent past.

If you are newly retired and have good professional clothes that you no longer plan to wear, many communities have "Dress for Success" programs that help outfit lower-income job applicants. Suitable clothing can be expensive for people just beginning to earn a salary. If no formal program exists, try contacting local migrant or immigrant organizations, rescue missions and rehabilitation programs, or Social Services. Local churches may also know of specific individuals who could benefit from your business clothing, or know of families needing other types of clothes.

The Woman's Alliance is a national organization whose focus is to provide business attire for women in need. Their Web site, www.thewomensalliance.org, is currently "under construction" but will have links to local organizations in the future. Meanwhile, if you go to Google, and type in "Donate Business Clothing" and your city or state, some local organizations may be listed.

Computers and Electrical Appliances

While most charities will accept small appliances that are in good , working order, they do not want computers. This is an item for which it is becoming harder and harder to find a home. In part, it is because they become outdated quickly through upgrades and new models, and it may be impossible to buy software, a compatible printer, and other peripherals for a computer that's 10 years old.

When George, a friend of Judi and Tom's, replaced his entire system, he wanted to find a place for his older computer and laser printer, which, though 11 years old, still worked well, if slowly. He called a local computer repair company, whom he had used several times, to see if they could suggest a recipient. They could not but suggested he might try his school district. When he did, he found that they had just upgraded the student-use computers and were looking for homes for *their* older ones. The computer director at the high school was investigating some possibilities in the community but had no room to store George's along with their own.

By mentioning his dilemma to friends, George was able to find a parochial school that could use his system, and gratefully donated it to them. In some areas, churches and nonprofit organizations still may be able to use a computer and printer. But more and more of them have purchased their own or already have a computer and peripherals donated from a member.

Another part of the problem is the complexity of using computers. With a secondhand TV or hair dryer, you can plug it in and know immediately if it works and how to use it. But with a computer, especially if you are new to this electronic world, when you turn it on, there is a bewildering array of icons and commands to learn. Internet access may require a separate modem for older models and a different kind of knowledge. When the novice runs into problems, it is impossible to know whether it is his own ignorance or a glitch in the system. There is no one to call the way there is with new computers still under warranty.

Does your nearby landfill need another computer and peripherals? Absolutely not. And some communities will not let you put it in the trash or will charge a fee for disposal. But if you have looked for creative solutions and have no other options, you may not have a choice.

Curios and Oddities

While not necessarily useful, these are items that make life more decorative and interesting. If you can hold out timewise, most of these do best at sales sponsored by the PTA or other community organizations. Many churches have sales with "white elephant" tables, and local historical societies may have an annual auction or sale. If it is not yet time for the sale, go through your home and stick a red dot on everything you wish to donate. When the time comes, you will be able to find them quickly.

As mentioned, drama groups are often looking for period clothing but can also use colorful props such as vintage luggage, older framed paintings and pictures, statuary, etc. They can also use fabrics to create backdrops.

Eyeglasses and Hearing Aids

When most people think of the Lion's Club, they think of donating old glasses, but not everyone knows that the Lions began sponsoring vision projects after Helen Keller challenged them to become "knights of the blind in the crusade against darkness" at their International Convention in 1925. Eyeglasses, which can be deposited in containers in libraries or community offices, at Goodwill shops, or at Lenscrafters, have their exact prescription read by a machine. They are labeled and stored until they are a match for a patient, often in a developing country. You can find more information at www.lionsclubs.org.

Hearing aids can be mailed in a padded envelope to Hear Now, 6700 Washington Avenue South, Eden Prairie, MN 55344. You can learn more about the organization by calling 800-648-HEAR (648-4327).

Fur Coats

Many of us had mothers to whom the ultimate luxury was owning a fur, preferably a full-length mink. Many of our mothers realized their dream. Unfortunately, it may not be ours. But it is not unfortunate if you are looking for another life for a fur you may have inherited but do not want to wear. You can donate it to PETA (People for the Ethical Treatment of Animals) and request that it be used as bedding for orphaned baby animals that are being raised in wildlife shelters until they are strong enough to return to their habitats. You can mail the fur to PETA, 501 Front Street, Norfolk, VA 23510, or telephone 757-622-PETA (622-7382) for further information.

Furniture and Household Goods

Donors are sometimes chagrined to learn that charities don't want their threadbare sofas or well-worn mattresses, that they will accept only items in salable condition. If you are calling an organization to pick up your furniture, make sure it meets their criteria. The manager of a Salvation Army thrift store told us ruefully that when she refused a broken convertible sofa missing two of its cushions, the caller yelled at her, "But you're a charity! You're supposed to take everything!" and banged down the phone.

If you have furniture and household goods in decent condition, you can also contact homeless and battered women's shelters because their residents usually need items to set up a new household. They can especially use linens, towels, and bedding. If you aren't sure where to find these groups, contact your local Social Services agency, asking to speak with someone in public relations. Habitat for Humanity also accepts appliances 3 years old or newer, new lighting, plumbing, and building supplies. What they don't use directly, they sell very reasonably in the community for the proceeds. Most of their ReStores keep a wish list of items people need or want to buy, which is matched up with those of donors.

Medical Equipment

Although organizations do not accept medications from individuals, there is a need for larger items to use both at home and in developing countries. These include wheelchairs, walkers, canes, motorized scooters, power wheelchairs, and hospital beds. Here are two agencies you can contact:

Clear Path 206-780-5964. Located in Washington State, they provide equipment for land-mine victims.

The Multiple Sclerosis Society. Contact your local branch, listed in the telephone directory, to make donations.

Musical Instruments

As long as music is taught in the schools, there will always be a place for a flute, viola, trumpet, or other instrument in good condition. Many school districts will accept instruments directly. Some others will ask you to donate them through the rental store that supplies them to the school. Your community may have the equivalent of San Diego's "Save the Music" foundation (866-968-7999), which facilitates the donation or exchange of used instruments.

Pets

Because they'd had a wonderful experience with two Siamese cats, a father and then his son, years later, Judi said to Tom, "You know what? I'd really like another male Siamese."

The next night, they were having dinner with friends when the husband, Mike, suddenly asked, "You don't know anyone who wants a male Siamese cat, do you?" His mother was entering assisted living and could not bring her 10-year-old cat with her.

When Tom and Judi met Thai, they fell in love with him and had six wonderful years together. He was an amazing cat who knew how to use the toilet and retrieve objects like a dog would. The point? Don't assume that an animal is "too old" or that everyone wants puppies or kittens. People who are experienced with pets understand that providing a home for a beloved older animal is more important than the gratification of knowing he will be with you for a long time.

If you cannot find a home for a pet yourself, choose a shelter that actively adopts out animals, even if you need to make a donation to do so. These are listed in the yellow pages, usually under "Animal Shelters" and often state their policy, such as "No kill since 1923." As far as the fear that an older pet will not adjust to a new owner, most animals who have been well treated adapt very well.

When Judi's mother moved to assisted living and had her own suite, she was able to bring her wire-haired terrier, Max. Gradually, as her illness progressed, she lost interest in him, and he was adopted by one of the staff members, who was thrilled to have him.

Suitcases

Now that luggage with its own wheels has replaced earlier varieties, you may feel that your older canvas luggage and hard-shell suitcases are obsolete. But consider donating them to your local Social Services agency. Far too many children enter foster care or move from one home to another with all their clothing and possessions in black garbage bags. The symbolism does little for their self-esteem. A suitcase in good condition would send a different message.

Vintage Dolls

If you have an established collection, you will no doubt sell most of them or give them to family members, but for those that are not in good shape, consider a doll hospital. Sometimes they will repair the dolls and donate them to charities to be sold. But even if they are simply being used for parts, you are extending their usefulness.

RECYCLING/TRASHING

All garbage is not created equal. You probably know that already. But until you start actively disposing of items, you may not have thought much about what goes where. Most communities already have recycling programs for newspapers, cardboard, metal, and plastics with the recycling symbol and have a "waste management" booklet available that spells out exactly what you can and cannot do. Look for the "Did You Know?" box for general regulations, but consult your own local government if you are not sure. Some communities will pick up remodeling and construction debris, but not if a professional contractor is involved.

The Inspiring Dumpster

When we mention the word dumpster in our workshops, people laugh nervously—who would want the neighbors to know they have *that* much stuff? Yet we believe most people could benefit by renting a dumpster once every 10 years or so and definitely when they are remodeling or scaling down. Participants begin considering the idea more seriously when we point out that some of what they may have in the basement or spare room are old, bulky items that were put there when they bought new furniture and didn't know what to do with the old—and still don't. Maybe you thought that if you put the stained sofa in the basement with the other clutter, family members would mistake the area for a rec room.

Part of the problem is that certain pieces of furniture simply go out of style for the time being. Think about studio couches that, even when they were popular, felt awkward to sit on and had an alarming way of suddenly sliding out from the wall. Add to them maple platform rockers, formal secretaries with tiny pull-down "desks," large stereo or TV consoles, warped Ping-Pong tables, bulky bassinets, and whatnot shelves that look much too ornate for current tastes.

When Judi rented a container recently for some remodeling, her next-door neighbors, a vigorous couple in their early eighties, coined the term "the inspiring dumpster." And it was. She invited them to use it, and they realized it was a golden

---

RECYCLING WISDOM

You may not realize all the options you have for recycling household goods.

- *You can dispose of latex paint cans in your garbage pickup, but the paint must be dried out.*
- *Household batteries are acceptable in the garbage, but those that are nonalkaline (those used in hearing aids, cell phones, watches etc.) should be taken to a recycling center—along with old car and boat batteries.*
- *The pages from books are acceptable to be placed in paper recycling bags, but the binding and covers must be removed first.*
- *Motor oil is not allowed in curbside pickup but can be dropped off at any auto repair or gas station that does oil changes.*
- *Smoke detectors and tires with their rims removed may be placed in curbside garbage, but deceased animals should be brought to a landfill for a fee or disposed of by calling the municipal animal shelter.*
- *The following are considered pollutants and should be brought to a special municipal facility: lawn and garden products, automobile fluids, oil-based paints and strippers, toilet bowl cleaners, silver polish and room deodorizers, oven cleaners, swimming pool chemicals, pesticides, carpet cleaners, kerosene, and anything else that could harm the environment by getting into the ground and then the water supply.*
- *Ceramics, mirrors, and glass should be wrapped securely, taped, and labeled "Glass" even if not broken.*
- *Most communities will pick up scrap metal such as appliances, boat trailers, bicycles, etc. by appointment, or they can be taken to the landfill free of charge.*
- *Small appliances such as microwave ovens, TVs, and vacuum cleaners can be placed in the regular garbage.*

opportunity to get rid of things they had been holding onto "just in case." Judi was likewise inspired. Although she had felt their large basement was well organized, the contractor thought otherwise. When he came to assess the situation before adding ceiling tiles and a lighting system—to complete its transformation into an art studio/darkroom/tool workshop/laundry area—he looked around and said dismissively, "You've gotta get this stuff away from the walls." The "stuff" included old family sporting equipment such as a roof rack that could hold four bicycles, a mattress and bed set from her in-laws' home that Tom had not wanted to part with, mismatched tables holding art supplies—you get the picture.

A dumpster was the way to go. Judi went through the rest of the house looking for those things that were inoffensive but not worth donating and were no longer loved. Her neighbors shredded stacks of papers to bring over. In 2 days, the container was full and taken away. We have seen this kind of inspiration strike in other situations. A lot of questionable items—rusty lawn furniture that could be refurbished but hasn't been, old rugs, nonworking lawn mowers, 20 years of files for a defunct organization, outgrown Ping-Pong tables and other hangers-on—find their way into it. As long as the container is there, you want to get your money's worth, and you might not have another such opportunity anytime soon. The dumpster's presence inspires you to sort through and get rid of things you might not have otherwise.

"Bring Me One of Those . . ."

How do you get a dumpster in your driveway or at your curb? If you have a private garbage company, call them, and they will supply the size you want for as long as you want it. Otherwise, you can use the yellow pages to look up "Rubbish and Garbage Removal." A lot of the ads you'll see will mention rental units. Since the sizes are calculated in terms of "yards," discuss with the company what you plan to dispose of, and ask them to suggest a size. Then get one a size larger! We prefer the convenience of the walk-in type to those where you toss the items over the side, but other people enjoy the catharsis. Expect to pay around $250 for a company to deliver an empty dumpster and haul it away full.

The amazing thing is that most people, even after passing along treasures to family and friends, selling things, and making donations to charity, still have enough to fill a dumpster. But that's what scaling down is all about.

"THIS IS YOUR LIFE!"

When we were growing up, one of TV's most popular shows was devoted to surprising individuals—from the famous to the merely well-known—by suddenly pouncing on them and announcing, "This is your life, _____ _____!" The dazed celebrity would be led to a chair, and from behind a curtain would gradually emerge his parents, Sunday school teacher, college roommate, and so on, usually preceded by their voices giving clues.

"Hi, Ralphie. You were my first student to bring in a boa constrictor for show-and-tell."

"Is that Miss Griggs? My kindergarten teacher? I don't believe it!" Ralphie would gasp and then be embracing her a moment later.

As children, we were amazed at how they were able to locate these ancient people after so much time. The adults seemed to enjoy the reunions. People love a good story. Yet a lot of the time, we don't know our own family's stories. We have only a handful of facts and anecdotes about our grandparents and great-grandparents, a few photographs, perhaps, but no real narrative. And what we do know, we don't always think to pass along to our children or nieces and nephews. We also forget that succeeding generations may want to know more about *us*.

If you have already placed things that you feel are important about you in a Memorabilia Box and have a collection of sorted photos, you have a good start. What you need to do next is put them together in a Life Book, a collection of information, photographs, and memorabilia about yourself. This is not one of those premade albums on the order of "Grandma Remembers" or similar titles, by the way. Even if we are grandparents, most of us don't think of that as our primary role. Those books have a feeling of looking back from an already completed life; we're still vital people with some of our best adventures ahead of us. The books have spaces that may not apply and that we would have to leave blank. Most have only places for writing down happy memories and successful events and do not allow space for the real lives that most of us have lived.

GETTING OVER THE OBJECTIONS

The thought of trying to put your life down in black and white can be terrifying. Your first thought may be, "That's a good idea—for someone else!" But before you exclude yourself by using one of the excuses below, consider the ideas that follow them.

"There's too much! I couldn't possibly fit everything about my life in one album."
If you feel intimidated by what it would encompass, ready to give up before you get started, remember that it's up to you to put in as much or as little as you want. Even if you just include pictures of your parents and grandparents, copies of your birth certificate and marriage license, some photos with identifications of who's in them, and a report card or two, that is probably more than you know about your own grandparents and great-grandparents. Don't let perfectionism get in the way of a worthwhile gift to the future.

If you're thinking, "I want to do it right or not at all," realize that there is no wrong way to do it.

"There are things I don't want to talk about, that I don't want people to know."
Unlike the picture-perfect narratives on "This Is Your Life!" real lives are a whole

lot messier. There are divorces, deaths, relationship ruptures, failures, job and money losses, illegitimacies, family traumas, health tragedies, breakdowns, and just about anything else you can think of. Life has taught—and is still teaching us—lessons. To be truly alive is to make mistakes. As one friend put it, "Having a perfect image is so not what life is about."

Still, in this album you can pick your level of candor. If you intend to keep the album to yourself during your lifetime, it will be very freeing to look back at everything that has happened and see yourself at various stages of life. If you want to skip various parts of the past that are still too painful or embarrassing, that is completely up to you. You may come back to them later—or never.

"I don't have time for this."

This is not an impressive excuse. If you keep the television off one night a month and spend 2 to 3 hours working on your album, it will take shape quickly. You don't have a deadline to meet, and you'll soon get to the place where you are enjoying it so much that you want to spend more time and become more elaborate. It is even the type of project you may want to do with several friends, the way people "scrapbook" together.

"Can't I just write the story of my life?"

Of course you can. But as anyone who has tried it will tell you, it is difficult to keep going after you have jotted down a few childhood reminiscences. You will need to be persistent and organized to get through the process. Even if you persevere, it may be daunting for other people to try to read several hundred pages of handwritten material. In a Life Book, documents and photographs give a framework and prompt your memory, and you can do as much writing as you want.

"I don't have anyone who would be interested."

Even if you are single, an only child with no cousins or other relatives, you probably have a close friend with younger family members. People are interested in the life story of someone they know, especially if it includes photographs and is done in an interesting way. Even if you think you have no one to leave it to, do it for yourself.

A few years ago, there was a sad letter in Ann Landers' advice column. A woman wrote in that she had been keeping a series of diaries for years with the idea of leaving them to her son, but he had died, and there was no one else interested. She was on the verge of throwing them all away. Ann Landers encouraged her not to do that, pointing out that such documents would have value in the future and to consider leaving them to an historical society instead.

"I don't know how to make a Life Book or where to start!"
Creating an album is what the rest of this chapter is about. Based on making our own books, we will take you step-by-step through the process. This is not only for women, by the way. In the past, every great man wrote his memoirs. Depending on your circumstances, you can also help an older relative make a Life Book or, if appropriate, create one for them. When Judi's mother was in assisted living, and her memory was failing, family members created a simple book for her with the photographs of familiar people and places. She looked at it until it wore out.

FINDING AN ALBUM

Thanks to the emphasis on scrapbooking over the past 10 years, it is much easier to find an archival album, one that is acid-free and lingon-free. That means that the materials will not discolor or disintegrate the contents over time. A sad contrast are the albums with self-stick pages and clear plastic overlays, whose glue strips will quickly brown and bond with your material, making it impossible ever to remove anything without damage. The best-size album is 12 inches by 12 inches with plastic sleeves into which you can insert completed pages and easily take them out and move them if necessary. Refill pages and plastic sleeves can be bought and easily added. In the future, if you want a different cover, the entire collection of pages can be moved. Pioneer is a brand we often recommend to our clients.

Best of all, these albums are not hard to find. Most people have at least one craft or scrapbook store in their area, and you can find them in the yellow pages. If not, there are many companies that offer a variety of interesting styles over the Internet. Either you or a helper can go to Google and type in "scrapbook albums" to bring up sites such as Stampington.com or Twopeasinapod.com. If you want the album embossed, try Exposures or Light Impressions. Both companies also make catalogs. See "Scrapbook Sources" below for contact information.

GETTING CREATIVE

If you look at a scrapbook site on the Internet or go into a specialty store, you will be dazzled by the many background papers, stickers, and embellishments used to make creative pages. You may want to go that route; if you do, you will find it exhilarating. Many books have been written giving examples and sample layouts and are available in libraries and bookstores. But our primary purpose is to put these pages together to make a record of your life, and a package of black 12 by 12-inch pages will work just as well.

SCRAPBOOK SOURCES

More and more communities now have specific scrapbooking stores and arts and craft centers that carry a lot of the materials you will need. They often give classes on putting memory books together. If you don't have a convenient retail store, you can also check out the following national and Internet resources:

Michaels, The Arts and Crafts Store. Stores in many areas and also online at Michaels.com

Jo-Ann's Fabric Store. Stores across the country and online at joann.com

Exposures. Albums and archival materials available by catalog (request it at 800-222-4947)

Light Impressions. A catalog of albums, papers, and display ideas that can be ordered by going to their Internet site at www.lightimpressionsdirect.com or by calling 800-828-6216.

Stampington.com. A wonderful Internet source for everything you can imagine. They also publish several related magazines such as *Legacy* and *Somerset Studio.*

Scrapbook.com. An Internet store devoted to scrapbooking with page layout ideas and hints as well as supplies.

Note: There are hundreds of Internet sites that would be able to help you. Just go to Google, and type in "memory book."

When you buy your album, you will also need to get a roll of "adhesive dots." These go on the back of items and are strong enough to hold them firmly in place, yet let you remove something if you want to do so. As far as narrative information is concerned, you can write it on the computer and print it out or simply hand write it. Various-colored index cards work well for the purpose.

THE EASIEST WAY TO START

When you have the necessary items gathered together, there will inevitably come a moment of paralysis. The blank pages seem perfect and forbidding. You do not feel adequate to the task. Whose bad idea was this, anyway? But the good news is that, unlike traditional bound albums, with this type, you can remove pages from their sleeves and redo them any way you want. You can start with more recent events if you wish and put everything in chronological order later. If you feel reluctant to use original photos, you can scan them into your computer and print them on photographic paper or put several on a page and color-copy them at your library or an office supply store. That way you will feel freer to cut them up and arrange them.

Although the album may include other people along the way, it is primarily about your life. For once it is unashamedly "all about you." Every Life Book will be different, of course, but here are some general categories and labels for sections to get you started.

CATEGORIES

Forebears. The relatives who are familiar to you—your parents, grandparents, aunts, and uncles—will seem more and more exotic through time. Go back as far as you can with names, dates if you know them, and a few representative photographs or other mementos. If you don't feel you have time to write something about them now, leave a blank area or index card so you can come back later and add information. You will, of course, have more information about your parents than more distant relations.

In the beginning. Most of what goes here can be self-explanatory. Your birth or christening certificate, an announcement, baby pictures, a photograph of your first home. If you don't have a picture but can go back and take one, do so.

Early childhood. Photographs and any paper memorabilia, sample artwork, your name as you printed it on a book or a greeting card, reproduced on a copier if necessary. Later on, you may want to look at magazines or newspapers from those years—available at large public and university libraries—and add photocopies of favorite toys or foods.

Siblings. Information about them and a few photographs of them at different ages and some strong or funny memories. You don't need too many.

School days. Any class pictures, photos of your schools and activities, or report cards. If you hated school or school lunches or school activities, by all means say so. Your descendants will appreciate your being candid.

Teenage years. This may be a large section, since it was an emotional time for many people and seemed to go on for so long. This is a good place to include photos of your friends and dates with brief notes about them, though not necessarily lumpy objects like pressed corsages or athletic letters. Use photographs instead.

College or first career. Although you were probably still a teenager, this is a new stage and can be treated that way.

Marriages or relationships. These days, many people have been married more than once or had significant relationships that were like a marriage. By grouping them together, this section can reflect your history without having to give long explanations or assessing blame.

Memorial pages. Part of life is losing someone who is dear to you, whether it is a sibling, child, parent, or someone else whose passing was a loss. The entire page or pages can have photographs, a description of the person, and your feelings about them.

Adult life. At this point, you may want to divide the pages up by decades or by experiences if, for instance, you lived in different places. Or, you may want to continue by category.

Career. You will probably have more memorabilia here than photographs. But the most important thing is writing how you felt about your work, and what you feel it accomplished.

Children. You can have photographs and descriptions at various ages of your own children or any others who are important to you.

Travel. If you go away frequently, you no doubt already have photo boxes or albums of your trips. This category is not to duplicate those but to pick out one or two photographs, postcards, or pieces of memorabilia about your trips, and write a paragraph of your impressions and feelings.

Pets. People who love cats or dogs usually have a number of them over a lifetime. Grouping the pictures together and writing a brief, funny or heartwarming anecdote about each can lift your spirits when you look at the pages.

Homes. It may feel especially important to you to photograph your current environment if you will be moving and even some of your things before you give them away. If you have lived in a number of places and have the pictures, it will also be interesting to you to see how your tastes have evolved.

Avocations. A nice, old-fashioned word that means your interests. You can include photographs of your garden, your artwork, yourself playing tennis, your postcard collection, or anything else. Also write down how you feel/felt when doing it.

Friends. If you have some long-term friendships, it is fun to put photographs of when you first knew them next to current pictures. You don't need to include every friend you have or had, however.

Spiritual life. Your practices may have evolved from a traditional religious background to a broader interpretation or some other form entirely. You may either want to identify your current beliefs or briefly trace their evolution, including everything from a church bulletin to a scanned dust jacket of one of Deepak Chopra's books.

Favorites. Most people feel strongly about what moves them, whether these are favorite books, works of art, music, movies, or people they regard as heroes. You may want to photograph book jackets or record albums and include art reproductions and photographs. Or you may just want to make a list. If what you respond to are scenes from nature and being outdoors, include images of those.

A letter to future generations. This can be addressed to your own descendants or the world at large, expressing your hopes and good wishes for them.

The key to a successful Life Book is balance—not overdoing one category and skimping on the others. On the other hand, even putting a few pieces of papers together or not completing the album is better than not doing it at all. Whatever you do, it will not be wrong.

SHOP TILL YOU DROP...OUT

The only time Judi was ever at a loss for words was during a question-and-answer period when she was speaking to an audience of affluent young women. One of them raised her hand and asked urgently, "What I really need to know is how to organize my shopping receipts for the things I'm going to return."

There was an immediate murmur of agreement.

Not being a career shopper herself, Judi was stunned to realize that an entire audience could have so many things to return to stores that they could not easily keep track of them. Even though she and Marj joked about "retail therapy," this seemed to take shopping to a new level.

Yet it should not have been a surprise. In a fascinating book, *Affluenza,* by John de Graaf, David Wann, and Thomas H. Naylor, the authors quote a 1998 poll in which 93 percent of teenage American girls rated shopping as their favorite activity. No wonder: There are twice as many shopping centers as high schools in the United States, and more people visit shopping malls each week than attend church.

Not you, of course. In an unscientific study, most people queried said they *never* go to the mall. Many even felt that shopping was not an important part of their lives. Yet it gives meaning to daily living in ways we may not think about. There is a sense of purpose in having to buy groceries for dinner, find a dress for a wedding, look at cars when we need to replace one.

If you are a recreational shopper or someone who gets a lot of pleasure out of wandering through stores and buying whatever is too much of a bargain to pass up, we are not going to try to change you. Well, we might try, but only by looking more closely at habits and motivations, and by suggesting alternate activities. If you are happily scaled down at this point, you will not want to start overcrowding your life again with stuff.

Getting back to our group of shoppers with too many receipts: The suggestion that they put each receipt in its bag with the item, put the bags next to the door, then return them all at once was met with objections. They hadn't yet decided whether or not to keep the things. Having piles next to the door or in the car would look messy. Besides, many were catalog purchases that would have to be mailed back. Having had clients whose dining room tables were littered with mail order returns several years old, Judi suggested that they file all their receipts in one place, by date. That way they could at least see when purchases were close to the return expiration point.

But of course, there was much more going on here than purchasing the necessities of life. These 30- and 40-somethings were in the process of building an identity, creating status, and, in a few cases, self-medicating. Being able to discuss their finds with each other and give one another tips and suggestions enhanced social interaction and created a group dynamic. Many had yet to realize what a burden too much stuff can be.

THE SHOPPERS' CLUB

People have always gravitated toward others with similar interests. The interest is sometimes a shared activity such as quilting or golf and sometimes an attitude based on which newspapers you read, whether you love football or helping others, or share the same spiritual beliefs. There is a sense of camaraderie, a feeling that you understand the other person and have topics to talk about that are meaningful to both of you.

There are people whose relationships are based on the shared activity of shopping as well. These are the people who say, "We're going to London and shop till we drop!" and for whom the highlight of their vacations is coming home and showing each other what they found. They take bus trips together to famous outlet towns. One TV quiz show featured two lifelong friends who accompanied their husbands on business trips so they could shop during the day when the men were in meetings.

If you believe that there are mostly women in this club, you are probably right. Male shopaholics usually travel by themselves, not in packs.

All recreational shoppers do not head for the mall. Perhaps you are addicted to garage sales or flea markets and, with your friends, make the rounds every weekend. Perhaps your spouse is the one who enjoys the circuit, and you go along to keep her company. What's wrong with *that?*

There is nothing wrong with shopping for fun. Just as having too much clutter is not "sinful," buying things is not a moral issue unless you are harming someone else by going into debt. But it takes great discipline to not bring home "treasures" on impulse. If you are committed to living happily in a smaller space, it means getting rid of a similar item.

Ever since he retired, Harry has loved going "saling" as he calls it. His stated purpose is to rescue old municipal maps and blueprints that he feels are an underrated part of local history. Once in a while, he makes a real find in that area. But he rarely returns empty-handed. His interest has expanded to old globes that show now-obsolete countries, brown gooseneck desk lamps, and anything else he feels is unique and at risk of disappearing. So far, he has kept his collection in one corner of the garage, but his wife wonders what will happen when they move permanently to their beach condo.

We maintain that it is impossible to spend a morning attending estate and garage sales without being tempted into buying something you had not planned on. So why place yourself in harm's way?

GET OUT OF THE LOOP

This is the loop of browsing, buying, telling people what you've bought and what you want to buy next. When Lily retired as a school nurse, it took her several months to identify what else was pleasantly missing besides her job. "I realized that in the teachers' lounge, there were two main topics of conversation: food and shopping. Everyone was always on a diet and talking about food. Then someone would ask where the best place was to get a pair of sandals, and everyone would have a resource. A lot of information was passed around, and everyone could join in. Now I love the silence."

GOING COLD TURKEY

Shopping may not be a way of life for *you*. But even in our workshops, when we make the suggestion "Stay out of stores for a month, including malls, garage sales, discount warehouses, craft fairs, eBay, and the shopping channels," the idea is greeted with nervous laughter. What we have just suggested is unthinkable. Why would we propose anything so drastic? Do we want to ruin the economy?

There are several reasons why we suggest going cold turkey for a month.

Exposure Creates Desire

Exposure creates desire. This is so crucial that it bears repeating. Exposure creates desire. This is the way it works: You may not have anything very specific in mind when you go to the mall or stop at a yard sale or begin browsing on eBay. Then you spot a bargain that is too good to pass up, at a price so low that it would be irresponsible *not* to buy it. Even though you already have flannel bed sheets or a serviceable windbreaker, you may never again see any as good as these for 50 percent off their original price.

Or you come across some ingenuous new electronic gadget you did not even know had been invented. Perhaps you see a beautiful one-of-a-kind piece of art. Even though you had no idea of its existence when you woke up that morning, you suddenly feel that owning it will make you happy and that not having it will

(continued on page 176)

9 BAD REASONS TO GO SHOPPING

1. "My car inspection will take an hour or two. I'll just ask them to drop me off at the mall."

Using shopping as a time killer is like lighting a match next to a gasoline can; even though it may not be a disaster, nothing good can come of it. If you know you are going to have to wait, make a plan. Bring along bills to pay, a book to read, a guidebook to plan your next vacation.

2. "I only need to spend another $36 to earn enough miles for my trip next month. It doesn't even matter what I buy; I'll be saving more money by the free flight."

If you need another charge on your credit card in a hurry, use it at the supermarket to buy groceries or fill up the gas tank or pay a bill. You don't have to purchase an extracurricular item.

3. "I'm going to start my Christmas shopping early."

Yes, there are people who can buy gifts far ahead. But the rest of us need to be sure that it is something the recipient will still want 6 months from now. We also need to avoid the pitfalls. You know the pitfalls. Many times when we are trying to shop for other people, we see things that *we* really want instead. When you buy a gift ahead of time, you also have to find a place to store it and remember for whom you bought the present.

4. "It's fun to bring back tangible reminders of our vacation."

This is the way many world-class art collections got started. Just make sure you are bringing home great paintings and sculpture and not kitsch. Okay, if you can't afford masterpieces, at least look for original crafts. Forget the reproductions of the Eiffel Tower and other mass-produced trivia, and don't fall into the trap of buying a lot because the prices are so reasonable in a particular country. Souvenirs you can actually use, such as linens, foodstuffs, or clothing is a better way to go.

5. "What an awful day! I really need a pick-me-up."

When it's been a bad day, the beckoning lights of the mall, the promise of novelty, the chance to focus on something besides your current circumstances all hold an appeal. It isn't terrible if you give in once or twice a year. But if retail mood-altering becomes a habit, you can end up with a lot more stuff—things that promised a quick fix, but just as quickly lost their appeal.

6. "I love to buy things for my grandchildren."

Yes, there are wonderful and unique things being made for children. But before you extract your credit card once again, picture their rooms as they are now. Most children's' rooms are overflowing with toys, stuffed animals, and adorable decorations. You also need to remember that it is as hard for some children to part with anything as it is for some adults. Chances are, when your children were little, you shopped for them mainly for their birthdays, Christmas, or Hanukkah. Think about doing the same for your grandchildren, with something irresistible thrown in only now and then.

7. "I'm not exactly sure what I want. But I can always take it back if it's not right."

Stores love this attitude; they know that once an item is in your possession, the chances are better than half that that is exactly where it will stay. Once you bring something home, it is easy to misplace the sales slip, forget the expiration date, or decide it is not worth the trip back to the store to return something under $10. Your thinking now changes to "I can always use it."

8. "When I retired, my office gave me a gift card to _____. I can't wait to spend it!"

Try to restrain yourself. While there is probably something you have been wanting, you do not need to spend the whole amount immediately. When Judi left social work, she was given a gift card for a department store. She bought a microwave oven that she is still grateful to have and some forgettable summer clothes that are long gone. If there's nothing you crave several months later, you can always use the card to buy holiday gifts.

9. "Everybody is getting those new dripless grills. I just want to take a look and see if they're as good as they say."

Beware of anything new that you did not independently think about wanting. There are just too many fad objects that "everyone" is buying. These may be used two or three times but do not become a part of your life. If you need to be reminded of what these are, take a walk in a thrift shop run by a charity, and look at the shelves filled with fondue pots, yogurt makers, crepe pans, nail polish dryers, electric hair curlers, and other items that were not that helpful in the long haul.

make you feel deprived. If it is a gift for someone else, you begin to imagine their excitement when they open the package, and their gratitude to you. By nightfall, it is yours.

"I'm Being Manipulated!"

If the item was store-bought, be aware that you did not stumble on it "accidentally." Advertisers, packagers, and retail buyers worked very hard to position it in the right place and make it appeal to you. You and your interests have been thoroughly researched and words and pictures carefully chosen to create the right emotional response. Even before you entered the store, they were expecting you.

This is not to vilify the retail industry; they are doing their job, often with astuteness and creativity. It is up to us to know that we are being conditioned to buy as many things as possible. Even the layout of a supermarket is planned in detail, set up so that you have to pass as many "optional" items as possible. A necessity such as milk is usually in the farthest corner from the door. By the time you reach the dairy case, the store manager is hoping that you have filled up your shopping cart with other "bargains."

You may have wondered why the large discount warehouses and shopping clubs have no express checkout lines. Our guess is that they see no reason to reward shoppers who buy only 10 to 12 items. These warehouses also do not identify their food aisles the way supermarkets do, no doubt hoping that shoppers will wander up and down all the rows, spotting items they hadn't realized they needed. Weather permitting, it would be fascinating to stand outside one of these warehouses for an hour and see the volume of goods in people's shopping carts—carts that are also oversized.

The High Cost of Bargains

Based on personal experience, we believe that it is impossible to spend a Saturday morning traveling around to various yard sales and not find at least one thing you need or crave. The prices are low, and there is the immediacy of having to buy it now or risk losing it forever. You do not have the option of going home and thinking about it overnight. Seeing a game from your childhood may create a rush of nostalgia that impels you to hand over 50 cents. And why not pick up a phone that works or an extra hammer or a beautiful decorator pillow for $2? After all, you never know . . .

This is a prime example of exposure meeting too-cheap-to-pass-up. It is a combination that is hard for most of us to resist. Many of the items are unique, so it is not a simple matter of going home and getting rid of something similar. Besides, going to tag sales or garage sales or yard sales or whatever they are called in your part of the country is recreational rather than necessary. You are looking for surprises, not shopping for a gallon of paint.

Since this kind of shopping is recreational, we had considered giving a list of alternate activities that you could do instead. But the trouble with such lists is that too often, they seem to be grasping for ideas. They suggest activities such as "Explore your community's history," as if you are back in the Scouts again, hoping to earn a merit badge. Few of us are looking for activities to fill up our time; our complaint is rather that there are too many things we want to do. The difficulty is often that the other things we want to do require supplies, planning ahead, and a certain energy and enthusiasm level to get started. It is easier to jump in the car and be entertained by someone else's stuff.

If this is your situation, take 10 minutes to sit down and list all the things you would like to do—take up ceramics, visit historic homes and gardens in the area, learn to rollerblade, write a memoir, buy a telescope and explore the stars, grow orchids, create something lasting for each grandchild, join Habitat for Humanity and help build houses—and so on. Listing them and thinking about how to accomplish them brings the activity a step closer. Then go for it! You'll be glad you did.

Why a Month?

When we suggest that people stay out of all retail venues "for a month," it is with the understanding that 4 weeks is a long-enough time to develop alternative behaviors. If a good habit can be set in place in 21 days, then another kind of habit should be able to be traded in for something better during that period. The problem with movements that promote "Turn off your TV for a week," or stop smoking for a day, is that a day or a week is not long enough for any meaningful change to take root. At best, you may enjoy the alternative and decide to continue it longer, but your behavior has not yet changed.

Another advantage of staying away from shopping for a month is that at the end of that time, you are able to look at your credit card charges or bank statement and be pleasantly surprised. It reminds you that you have a choice about how you want to spend your money. If you want a boost in this direction, read *The Millionaire Next Door* by Thomas Stanley and William Danko. The book gives an eye-opening look at how most of them found financial solvency by keeping a close look at *all* the money they spent.

SHOPPING PSYCHOLOGY

So far, we have been discussing the kind of shopping situations that are common to all of us. But there are other needs that buying things fill.

Shopping as Therapy

At a party recently, someone complimented Lori on her diamond earrings. "Thanks," she said and launched into a story about how she had gotten them on a shopping channel that had a "limited supply" at a wonderful price. Lori had recently undergone the breakup of a long-term relationship in which her lover had found a younger woman and moved out. "When I can't sleep, I switch the TV on. There are things I never expected to see for sale. You can get the best deals at 3 o'clock in the morning!"

She went on to say that when the package arrives, "It feels as though someone is sending me a wonderful gift."

Hopefully, as time passes, and her life regains its equilibrium, Lori will have less emptiness to fill with "stuff." Now she is trying both to fill a void in her life and to rebuild her lost self-esteem. The danger is that she may find herself hooked on the process and continue to buy long after she needs to do so.

Many people use shopping as a therapy tool in shorter bursts, as in . . .

"I'm feeling a little down; I think I'll go shopping."

Often, we don't even articulate how we are feeling. We feel restless or discontent or in need of inspiration and know that browsing through a store will improve our mood. At the least, it will provide distraction; at the most, a new image and an improved sense of ourselves. Instead of looking within to see what's going on, we hope that buying something that makes us look more attractive or successful or opens a new direction for us to travel in will give us a lift. A new dress or tie can suggest new adventure and an escape from the dreary routine. (But so can an exciting book from the library, doing something unexpected for someone else, or an inspiring phone conversation with a friend.)

Shopping to Belong

In an interesting study, *The Overspent American,* Juliet B. Schor identifies what she refers to in our lives as the "reference group": the people we respect and admire who set the standards to which we aspire. These people have aspirations and interests similar to ours—only better. Traditionally, these reference groups were made up of the people in our neighborhood or church or job. Now, through television programs and magazine advertisements, our "neighborhood" has greatly expanded. An interesting study conducted in 1991 by two researchers at the University of Florida, Susan Fournier and Michael Guiry, found that 85 percent of those interviewed aspired to be in the top 18 percent of American households. In contrast, only 15 percent said that they would be satisfied by "living a comfortable life."

One thing that makes the lifestyle of our expanded reference group seem similar to ours is their accessibility. Whereas few people identified personally with the Duke and Duchess of Windsor or other distant personalities, celebrities of the past 20 years such as Kelsey Grammar (playing Frasier), Jerry Seinfeld, Oprah Winfrey, or Hilary Clinton seem much more approachable—people with whom you could sit down and have a frappacino. Regis Philbin identifies himself as a "Bronx boy," and car owners in Mercedes ads look like the people standing next to you in the deli line.

Except, of course, they are millionaires, and the rest of us aren't.

The problem with having celebrities as your reference group is that you will never catch up. Once you have purchased the professional cookware and six-burner stove, there is still something missing. After a month or so, you purchase a convection oven and install a wine cellar. But now you need more sophisticated friends to entertain, and the celebrities in your reference group aren't *that* accessible, after all. So it's back to the mall to try something else.

Shopping as Image Enhancer

Sometimes, your reference group does not involve money as much as individuality and good taste. We want to be the only one in our immediate group—or at least the first—to have traveled to a particularly exotic place or own a breed of dog unknown to the world at large. We want to be considered unique—in an enviable way, of course, not as an eccentric. What can make trying to be individualistic a problem is when we depend on the external things we own to create our image, rather than having it based on the activities we do and love.

If your image is based on the uniqueness of how you dress or furnish your home, you will constantly have to update your look with something new. And unless you create a revolving door to get rid of the items that have become passé, you run the danger of a very cluttered life. Finally, unless you depend on advertising to let you (and several million other individualists) know what is the next unique thing, you will spend a lot of time browsing on your own.

Shopping as Refinement

If you have to shop, a better alternative is working to make your living space closer to what you want by refining what you have. The object of scaling down, after all, is to have only what you love or need. A harmonious room full of things you love lifts your mood when you walk into it and makes you want to spend time there. If the surfaces are filled with clutter, the room a jumble of furniture and items that you've never liked or are broken, it will make you uneasy. The appliances you own should work right and be pleasant to use and, of course, be *used*. It is better to replace a vacuum cleaner that is powerful but too heavy to carry around; find one that is light and easy to manipulate. If you feel like shopping, replace eight scratchy bath towels with four thick, fluffy ones.

Even this kind of shopping can be overdone if it feeds into a perfectionism that makes you obsessed with physical details. If you feel you are too focused on "getting everything just right," stop for a while. Take the one-month cure of avoiding shopping venues until stuff resumes its secondary role once more.

Still, the difference is that with this kind of shopping, you are working to make your own life better—not buying things to impress anyone else. When things are just the way you want them, then stop—it's as simple as that!

HOW TO KEEP
FROM CLUTTERING
YOUR NEW PLACE

A recent cartoon in the *New Yorker* showed five amoeba-like blobs milling around. One of them is looking at his watch and asking the others, "Time to head back?" The caption above the drawing was titled "Your Lost Weight." Although it would not have been as funny, the caption might also have read, "Your Old Stuff."

For anyone who hasn't already guessed, maintenance is the hardest part of keeping uncluttered. Scaling down is dramatic—emotional and exhilarating. You can see the results almost immediately; you feel wonderful in your re-created space. But if scaling down is a roller-coaster ride full of thrills and screams, maintenance is driving long miles on the New Jersey Turnpike.

Yet the news is not all bad. Once routines take hold, they become automatic. If you've trained yourself to always put your keys or your glasses in the same location, after a while, you will do it without thinking. The habit is reinforced every time you can locate them immediately. And once you do something automatically, it is no longer a burden.

To help you keep your home pared down, we've made a list of the most helpful things we have learned in years of organizing. If you adopt even one of these techniques, it will make your life easier. Two are even better. Take as many as you can use.

1. Have a wastebasket in every room. It doesn't have to announce itself; your "wastebasket" can be an inconspicuous wicker basket or a sleek metal cylinder, as long as *you* know what it's for. When you pick up a pen that no longer writes, you can quickly discard it instead of putting it back in the drawer with the hope that next time, it will be more cooperative. Even if you use the wastebasket for newspapers and magazines, you can move them into recycling bags later on. In the meantime, every room will look much more uncluttered.

2. Make sure that everything has a final resting place. Sounds ominous, but it only means that everything needs a home. Catalogs, shoes, screwdrivers, tablecloths, photographs, coupons, and everything else need a specific shelf, drawer, or folder where they belong. It makes life easier to know where to store something and where you can find it later on. Except for a tablecloth, for instance, the dining room table is not a valid address.

3. Return everything to its home. You *knew* this was coming. Even if you don't always put an item back immediately, knowing where it belongs makes cleaning up a quick task and ends the hassle of trying to remember where a particular thing was last sighted. Something in us resists putting the hammer right back when we've finished hanging a picture or returning the shoes we've just kicked off all the way to the shoe rack. We like to let a few of the groceries hang out on the counter for a while instead of stowing them immediately. As long as items get put away the same day, before they have a chance to be buried, there's no real harm done.

4. Pre-cycle paper. Don't bring home playbills, concert programs, church bulletins, museum guides, handouts from workshops, and so on. You have already experienced the event. You don't need visual cues to remind you of what you have just seen or heard.

5. Keep an ongoing medical chart. Compile a chronological list of all your illnesses, injuries, and operations, the year they occurred, and the treatment that was prescribed including specific names of medications. Add in the current medicines you take, even calcium and vitamins. It is easiest to put the information in one place on a computer. If you're not computer literate, ask a family member to do it for you—then print it out whenever you need to see a new doctor. If you're suspicious of machines, keep a printed copy for yourself. Writing it down in one place is easier than keeping a messy folder of forms and handwritten notes. Having the dates in front of you is helpful; as we get older, we tend to think that everything happened "last year."

6. Purge your periodicals. Pretend you're the magazine or newspaper delivery person who goes to supermarkets and stationery stores and takes away the previous issue when the new one hits the rack. Don't think about what articles you haven't read yet—you have a job to do.

7. Pick a number. Still on the subject of magazines, choose your two favorites, and subscribe only to them. Don't renew any others. Moving affords you a good opportunity not to fill out a change of address card for publications you no longer care about. Don't worry if you don't receive the last issues "coming to you"; your time is more valuable, as in this cautionary tale: George subscribed to a professional list over the Internet, and for a while, he found it helpful. But eventually the e-mails were taking too much of his time to read, and the other members' comments were often irritating. He spent a lot of time fuming over the list's stupidity. But because he had paid a year's dues, he felt he had to "get his money's worth" (about $8 at that point). So he let himself be annoyed for another 3 months.

8. Stop buying file cabinets. The usual reaction when a four-drawer file is full is to go out and buy another. But wait! What you need to do first is purge the contents of the files you have before you purchase more storage space. Remind yourself that 90 percent of what you file is never looked at again. Why save the tropical fish guides when you gave the aquarium away 5 years ago? If you are holding files for an organization that is now defunct, either ask around to see if anyone wants the material, or simply take the responsibility and declutter it yourself.

When Judi first started organizing workshops, she would ask participants to complete evaluation forms, indicating what they had found the most or least helpful, what they would like to hear more about, and the one thing that they planned to go home and do as a result of the program. The feedback was helpful in creating future presentations and the complimentary comments were flattering. But after a while, she had learned what she needed to know, and the stack of evaluations was a foot high. They had served their purpose and went into the recycling bag.

9. Form groups. If you haven't already done so, put items that are in the same category in one place: batteries, different kinds of glue, winter scarves, colored markers, and so on. You can purchase organizers for your gift wrap, bows, tags, tape, and a pair of scissors, but an empty drawer works just as well. So does a garment bag that can hold large rolls of paper and often has pockets you can use for the smaller items.

Keep all your bills, stamps, envelopes, and return address labels in the same section, all your vitamins conveniently in the kitchen. Grouping is an area that supermarkets and drugstores have mastered very well; department stores, on the other hand, often create confusion by having clothing organized by the maker. If you want a sweater, you may have to look in 10 different places. You can't control Macy's, but you can set up your home so that you only have one place to look.

10. Look at mail differently. It is our estimate that 95 percent of what comes in the mail wants your money: Bills, advertising flyers, catalogs, charity appeals, and coupons, to name the most demanding. Many magazines exist to sell you the products advertised. More than 40 billion catalogs are mailed out annually, approximately 150 for each American man, woman, and child, and the number of mailings from charities are even greater.

This is the most compelling reason that, when you bring in the mail, you should stand directly over the recycling bag, and drop most of it in. These companies and groups are not benignly sending you mail that they hope you will find interesting or entertaining; they are trying to find ever cleverer ways to make you part with your money.

11. Remember your favorite foods. If you enjoy takeout meals, keep the menus from nearby restaurants in a file folder next to the phone. Put a plus sign next to the dishes you've ordered and really liked, and a minus sign next to those that were a disappointment. Why make the same culinary mistake again? In the case of lengthy Chinese menus, highlight the numbers you like to order with a magic marker so that your eye will go right to them.

12. Limit your savings. Of plastic or brown paper bags, that is. These can take up a lot of space, as Marj found out when her client, Will, after some coaxing, sheepishly opened a kitchen closet door, and hundreds of plastic produce bags burst free. Not only were they taking up space that could be better used for kitchen staples, they were unnecessary. Flimsy plastic bags have no monetary value or enough use to justify their being hoarded. Paper bags are no longer used for book covers, but they can hold newspapers for recycling. A good rule is to limit your stash to whatever fits inside one plastic or one paper bag. When that bag gets filled, you can recycle the group and begin again.

13. "This one's for you." If you like to save newspaper or magazine clippings and cartoons for other people, put them in a folder, and give yourself a time limit. If you haven't sent them by the end of a month, realize that you won't, and recycle them. It is helpful to look at what is holding you back. If it is the feeling that you need to write a letter to go along with the clipping, buy a package of Post-its, stick one on with a sentence or two, and mail it.

When we go into homes, it is also common to come across shopping bags filled with items that people are keeping to pass along to a friend or relative or donate for a raffle. "I'm saving this tablecloth for my cousin, Betty. I have a round table now, and she always said how much she liked it."

"When are you going to see her?"

"Maybe next fall? She moved to Florida last year. But I want her to have it!"

"Why don't we box it up, and mail it to her?"

"Well . . . There's a stain I want to try to get out—and I haven't had time to do it."

If you are saving an item for someone you see regularly, put it in on your backseat where it is visible, rather than in the trunk where it can get lost again. Having it in sight will make you more anxious to move it out of your life.

14. Keep car things in the car. The following items can fit easily in your glove compartment: Your proof-of-insurance card, receipts for parts such as batteries and tires in case you need to get a replacement, directions to people's homes, maps, open-ended coupons for linen and craft stores, AAA contact information. In your trunk, it is a good idea to have a dependable flashlight, jumper cables, a white rag or distress flag, and flares. Even if you have a roadside assistance plan, you may find a thermal blanket, fire extinguisher, and first-aid kit (with wound closure strips, insect sting relief pads, scissors, and vinyl gloves) helpful in an emergency.

Put items you plan to return to stores and library books to go back in the car as well. That way, they aren't taking up space in your home, and you'll have them on hand when you find yourself near the library or mall.

15. Practice "one in, one out." By now, you know what that means. Get rid of that one-speed mixer, worn-out winter coat, or battered colander when you bring a new one home. Not only does it keep your space from getting cluttered again, there is something satisfying about the sense of making life better when you toss out a handful of stained and burned potholders in exchange for several attractive ones.

16. Take an evening work break. No, not a break from working in the evenings, a break from watching TV, reading, dozing, or otherwise relaxing. Before you go to bed, spend 15 minutes picking up and putting away. Set your timer if you want, and go through your area discarding old newspapers, hanging up clothes, wiping things clean. Just this small effort will give a fresh start to the next day and make you feel better.

17. Create permanent places for wanderers. The items most frequently lost include keys, glasses, TV remotes, and library books. Followed by pens, bills, socks, and poultry seasoning. If you carry a purse, have a definite place to set it down when you come in, and make sure your keys are with it or hanging on their own hook. Marj's daughter, Angelyn, bought a small decorated box at a yard sale for the TV remote control. It is pretty enough to double as a coffee table decoration, and they never leave the area without putting the remote back inside.

Some of us need glasses for distance, others for reading. If you aren't wearing glasses all the time, it's easy to put them down in the last place you used them and not remember where that was. Judi, who needs glasses for driving but rarely uses them in the house, learned from Marj to put them into a special holder. You can buy one made for the purpose—often brass and lined with felt—or use a ceramic mug or small container that you already have. Scaling down also means doing away with aggravation.

18. Beware of spares. Typical scenario: Your VCR still shows videos, but can no longer be programmed to record television shows. So you research VCRs and purchase a new one that works beautifully and does everything short of making popcorn. What happens to the old machine? Do you say a grateful farewell to it—or do you store it "just in case the new one breaks down," and you want to watch a movie?

Don't do it! Remind yourself that the reason you are replacing the old one is because it doesn't work right. Say goodbye to that semi-comatose appliance, along with the stained clothing you're tempted to add to your growing wardrobe of "work clothes," the hand mixer that was too lightweight to do anything but whip cream, the broom with broken bristles that you think you might use outside. Lose the bald tires lined up to use as "spares." Keep the old items for a couple of weeks if you have to, until you feel bonded to their replacements—then say goodbye.

19. Have appropriate containers and dividers. While we've seen people go overboard buying boxes and organizers, you do need to use some for particular items. This is especially true for clothing and accessories. Even if you only purchase a honeycomb-style divider that adapts to different drawer sizes and holds socks, stockings, or underwear; a scarf or tie hanger that has multiple openings and keeps them from wrinkling; and a hanging organizer with clear plastic pockets in which you can see jewelry at a glance, you will be ahead of the game.

Unless you live in the tropics, you'll need a specific place for gloves, wool scarves, and hats. If you have a closet near your front door, a plastic box or basket with these items can go on a shelf inside. In choosing containers, it also helps to think outside the box. Drawer dividers that are marketed for kitchen utensils or small tools are perfect for hair accessories, makeup, pens, and art markers, and can sit on a closet shelf.

If you like to send cards, a greeting card file will hold cards you purchase ahead of time in their proper month and have calendar spaces to write in birthdays, anniversaries, and other occasions. If you do buy cards ahead of time, having a file is especially important. Otherwise, you run the risk of having the experience of one of our clients, Diane. In sorting out her desk drawers, we unearthed years of unsent greeting cards. The only thing we could do about the ones beginning

"To My Dearest Husband on Our Anniversary" was laugh. Diane had survived an acrimonious divorce 4 years earlier.

20. Keep up your stock. That is, keep a generous supply of stamps, milk, computer printer ink, shampoo, toilet paper, and anything else you hate running out of. Part of organized living is to not become aggravated when you find you need something mundane and have to make a special trip to buy it. Unlike "spares" that sit around waiting for a tomorrow that never comes, these are staples that get used up and should be replenished. This also means keeping your car's gas tank well above the empty mark; just when you think you're settled in for the night, you may have to drive somewhere.

21. Consider the upkeep. Before you buy anything new, decide how much time you are willing to spend caring for it. You may initially feel that it doesn't matter, but linen slacks that need ironing every time you wear them, all-cotton tablecloths, white upholstered furniture, copper pots that need shining, and silver that has to be polished all cut into your precious time. They can also add pleasure to life, so choose wisely. If you love the look of sterling, for instance, choose that, and keep the rest of your life easy.

22. Follow a schedule. If you find you are starting to bulk up again, plan on filling one trash bag or can a week with household junk. If your garbage is picked up on a Thursday, for instance, plan on decluttering the night before and have it out by the curb. In Marj's condo, there is a shelf in the parking garage where people leave books, household items, or other "discards" so that anyone who wants to can take them. If they aren't gone in a week, they get trashed.

23. Visualize the outcome. When you consider adding something new to your life, first decide where you are going to put it. You may change your mind about purchasing another piece of exercise equipment when you realize there is no home for it except in the middle of your living room.

24. Go shopping without your credit cards. Even if you take cash instead, it changes the dynamic. A $20 bill in your wallet reminds you that you are spending money. If you are prone to impulse buying, not having a credit card will give you a cooling-off period to decide whether you really need or want the abs-firmer or a set of holiday dishes. If it still seems like a good idea the next day, you can always return to the store. Shopping without money is also a good idea at craft fairs and bazaars, where it is easy to get carried away—and carry away a hand painted sign that says, "Turtle Crossing," before you remember you have no front yard.

25. Never apologize. Never apologize about your home, that is. When you apply logic to the situation, it doesn't make much sense.

"I'm sorry the place is such a mess."

"Please excuse the way things look."

"Sorry that things are all over the place; I'm in the middle of sorting."

Think about it. Why are you saying you are sorry? Are you afraid that they have aesthetic sensibilities that will be offended by seeing things out of place? Do you feel you're letting down some world cleanliness standard or are personally insulting your visitor by not having everything pristine—you should have *known* they would be stopping by sooner or later. Does it show a lack of respect for who they are to make them stand in a cluttered hallway?

What you are really asking them is to not think badly of you, to excuse you from being judged and scorned by them. But why should you be? You are an adult, working out your own challenges. Scaling down is your goal, and you are on your way. Having too much stuff or being disorganized is *not* a moral issue. It won't even make you unpopular. We've never heard anyone say, "I can't be friends with them. Their garage is such a mess!"

26. Get over it. We all have preconceived ideas of how long something *should* take or how much you'll be able to do. We're taught that certain things should take a week or a month or a year and pace ourselves accordingly. Do all your holiday shopping in one day? Redo your basement in a weekend? Impossible, says conventional wisdom. And yet these things are done all the time.

When Chicago professor Karl finally scaled down his book collection, he was shocked that pulling out the books he no longer wanted and putting them in three piles—to toss, to take to the library for their next sale, or to take to a used bookshop to sell—took him less than an hour. It only took another hour to dispose of them and to "retire" the leftover metal bookcase that he had never liked. Two hours! "The anticipation was so much worse that the actual event," he said ruefully. "If I had known, I would have done it years ago."

27. Keep it inspirational. In a room you don't care about, which is dull or cluttered, it is easy to drop things anywhere and add to the disorder. When you take the time to decide a room's ambiance and work to have only what excites you in it, you will be much more motivated to keep it looking that way. Things that aren't put away or don't belong can look *very* out of place in such a room.

28. Have fun! When we talk about scaling down and getting rid of stuff as being fun, people often don't believe us at first. But when you are refining your life to make it closer to your ideal, when you are feeling control over your environment, it is exhilarating. Having a mission statement gives you a direction; it is up to you to make the process an adventure. When friends of ours, Bob and Pam, sold the large Victorian house Pam had lived in all her life, they shocked everyone by moving to a small, rundown farm in Virginia. Bob referred to it as "Our Last Great Adventure."

No doubt there were some painful moments in saying goodbye to lifelong neighbors and friends, in divesting themselves of ornate furniture and keeping only what they would use in a modest farmhouse, in negotiating the inevitable jolts and changes. Yet once they were committed to the plan, they had a great deal of fun along the way, and they are still having fun.

So should you!

part 5

THE REWARDS OF
LIVING LARGE

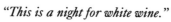

"This is a night for white wine."

STARTING
A NEW ADVENTURE

Judi rarely watched TV—until she discovered the Home & Garden channel and became a decorating junkie. For anyone interested in their environment, it was a smorgasbord of wonderful ideas. But once in a while, she would watch the program, "House Hunters," in which prospective buyers shop for a new home, and be appalled. Even first-time buyers on a budget would look at what seemed to Judi a normal-size bathroom or bedroom and say, "This is really *small.*" Or about a kitchen, "This looks a little *dated.*" As a friend who lives in a charming colonial home put it, "If they saw *my* bathroom, they'd run screaming."

Is this a normal reaction or one that is created by society? If left to themselves, would people think to junk a stove because it was last year's color or replace a refrigerator that spits out ice cubes but lacks a built-in water filtration system? A lot of this attitude appears to be created by conditioning, not independent thought. Although people spend less time in the kitchen cooking than ever before, they have been conditioned to demand enough counter space to host a nightly "Battle of the Chefs." Having large open spaces in the "master bedroom" is important because master bedrooms are *supposed* to be large. They are also supposed to have their own bathroom with double sinks and a Jacuzzi.

THE SIZE TRAP

Here's a quick way to tell if you have fallen into a supersized trap:

1. When eating out, you gravitate toward "Specials" that include appetizer, soup, salad, entrée, dessert, and coffee because they give you "more for the money" than just an entrée.

2. Given a choice, you would pick a three-car garage over one any smaller.

3. The less you use your kitchen for cooking, the more food processors and gadgets you seem to accumulate.

4. Though you always take showers, you crave a Jacuzzi tub.

5. Walk-in clothes closets are a necessary home feature.

6. When choosing a Christmas tree, you pick the largest one that can fit in the room.

7. A home on an acre lot is "better" than one on a quarter-acre.

8. The idea of a third-world family living in one room gives you chills.

9. You buy the huge package sizes at "warehouses" such as Costco, or B.J.'s or Sam's, even though you won't use up a gallon of Dijon mustard in this lifetime.

10. Your home has more TV sets than there are family members.

If you answered "yes" to two or more, you may have outsized expectations and need to examine your feelings about scaling down.

HOW BIGGER BECAME BETTER

The obsession with newness and hugeness invaded our living spaces many years ago and has trickled down from the very wealthy to those in modest financial circumstances. Hummers, SUVs, and supersize meals have helped create this mindset. It no longer matters that there are only three or four things you need to do in a bathroom or that the homes the "House Hunter" buyers are looking at often come equipped with huge living rooms, home office spaces, dens, and finished basements—making it unnecessary to have to set up a computer in a corner of the supersize master bedroom.

The Four-Car-Garage Personality

In case we've missed the link between size and personal status, advertising makes it for us. A state-of-the-art kitchen or a four-car garage tells the world how well you are doing. Even if you are not interested in impressing other people, living in a parklike setting reassures *you* that you are doing just fine. It is a compliment to your foresight and financial ability that you are able to own so much space, especially if it is well equipped. In earlier centuries in Europe, it was forbidden for anyone but nobility to wear certain kinds of clothing or own ornate furniture. You could actually be arrested and jailed for a gold-trimmed cloak if you were not "noble" enough to wear it.

Perhaps on some level, we are still rebelling against those strictures or at least responding to them, keying in to the part of the American Dream that promises that no matter how humble your beginnings are, if you are clever enough, if you work hard enough, you can make it big. Taking that expression another way, you can *physically* make it big. There is pressure to live up to your means, to demonstrate what is expected of a person of your status.

The Decline of Starter Homes

You may be surprised to realize that the idea of a "starter home" is an American invention. In Europe, most people stay in the same apartment or house for their adult lives; the property may have been handed down through their family, even if they lease rather than own it. Wealthier Europeans may purchase country homes or villas or seaside cottages, but most of them do not move every few years in order to keep trading up.

What *is* a starter home? The idea gained popularity after World War II with the Levittown development on Long Island that provided homes for returning soldiers; homes that were inexpensive to build and had basic rooms, small, flat yards, and no basements. Starter homes were not always located in the neighborhood to which their owners aspired. These houses did not have state-of-the-art appliances or enough rooms. It was understood that the young couples who lived in them were planning to move on.

Increasingly, the lines have become blurred. A first home now may not be everything a young couple wants, but it is larger and could actually be lived in comfortably for their lifespan. It usually has to have three bedrooms—a master, a guest room, and a home office that can be converted into a nursery—and at least two bathrooms. Starting out this way, when they decide it is time to move on, the only direction to move toward is supersize.

There is another reason that people feel it is necessary to move to a larger house. They have quickly accumulated more stuff and are looking for increased closet and storage space. The more storage their new home has, the more justification there is for owning as much as they do. With a walk-in closet the size of a second room, they'll not only be able to store everything they own but can also feel free to accumulate more. And before they move into it, they will not have to make painful decisions about what will go with them and what must be discarded.

When Judi and her family moved from a small rented cottage into her current home many years ago, the new space felt immense. There were three bedrooms upstairs, a basement, and a garage to spread out in. Then, faster than you can say, "I want that!" the space disappeared. It took a concentrated effort to scale the house back down to spacious. It is easy to fill space—we have all had student friends who furnished entire apartments with curbside finds—but harder to create your perfect environment.

Facing the Big Bias

If you are planning to live large in a smaller space, you are swimming against the tide. "Small" and "dated" are pejorative terms in our culture. You may be perfectly happy with your home—until someone exclaims, "What a cute little house!" and you feel insulted. Their comment has removed your home from being judged as normal-size and implied that you could not afford a full-size house or be able to decorate one. Perhaps it suggests that you are a "cute little person" for living in such a place.

Contrast that with how you would feel if someone said, "You have so much room!" or if someone told you, "You're so lucky to have a huge backyard!" The implication is that through your own cleverness and good management, you have been able to capture rooms and property. It doesn't matter to a lot of people if one person has a beautifully landscaped quarter acre or a well-appointed patio and another has an acre of jungle; or if the first has an inviting, cleverly used space and the second has 10 rooms crammed with junk. The larger is still thought to be advantageous.

So even though you have learned to differentiate yourself from your belongings and know that your self-worth does not depend on the size of your exterior environment, there will be moments when old feelings kick in. At those times, remind yourself that Mother Teresa will not be remembered for her walk-in closet or Jesus Christ for his four-donkey stable. To be less extreme, think about Benjamin Franklin and Agatha Christie, Michelangelo and the Beatles, who are remembered less for their luxurious homes than the contributions they made. This is not to go to the other extreme—the country would be poorer without Thomas Jefferson's Monticello or even Hearst Castle—but rather to try to divorce personal worth from physical size.

WHY SMALLER IS BETTER

There are solid reasons why it is easier to live large in a more manageable space. Great art and ideas have traditionally come from urban areas, where people live in small apartments and in proximity to one another. Many creative young adults head for cities, but more and more retirees are sacrificing lawns for the advantages of urban living. Aside from being part of an exciting culture, they are near research hospitals, public transportation, and other services. As one New Yorker pointed out, "You can get *anything* delivered to your door."

College towns have also become a choice for adults who are scaling down. Three years ago, Phil and Alana moved from a large house in the New Jersey countryside to an apartment in Princeton. They had been planning the move for a while and knew they would not be able to buy a comparable home and still be able to do all the things they wanted. Princeton offered the kind of life they were looking for. Like many universities, it allows residents to audit classes and attend cultural events on campus. "There's easy transportation to New York City," Phil explained, "and last year we took an archaeological study tour to Greece."

The six children they have between them had mixed feelings about their parents selling the house. After all, the house was large enough for several of them to come at once and crash for weeks at a time. The new apartment is not conducive to that. But their parents were ready for a change. Last Thanksgiving, they filled a bed and breakfast in Bucks County, Pennsylvania, which included the traditional feast. "Everyone had enough energy to take a walk afterward," Alana points out. "No one was exhausted from cooking the dinner and cleaning up."

In other college towns such as Ames, Iowa, Collegeville, Minnesota, and Davis, California, retirement communities are being created to take advantage of the universities and also offer empty-nesters the chance for the company of other interesting people. In Davis, for instance, an artist and writer had the opportunity to configure their 1,200-square-foot co-op apartment into a more open area and studio. It worked so well that the builders adopted it for other units.

Living on a Human Scale

Besides cultural opportunities, there are emotional advantages to living in a more compact space. Psychologists have found that people respond better to smaller rooms and spaces, finding them cozier and more comfortable to spend time in. Rather than settle down in large, high-ceilinged areas, people seek out alcoves, window seats, and niches to read, talk, or sip coffee in. In a restaurant, given the choice, most people choose a corner booth, preferably one with a high back. Studies have found that, as beautiful as they are, rooms with cathedral ceilings tend to be avoided when there is another option. At parties, instead of luxuriating in their spaciousness, guests pack together in the kitchen.

Think back to childhood and the pleasure you felt in a cardboard "house" or under the dining room table, or in a blanket fort or a tent. It was your own space, and the size felt exactly right. The truth is twofold: People can get along happily in much smaller spaces. People need a spot, especially if they live with other people, which is exclusively *theirs*.

A perhaps extreme example of cozy living is the Minnesota couple who live in a tree house situated on 5 acres, which they own. Built at first as a guest cottage, Will and Peggy Line loved it so much that they decided to move in themselves. They have plumbing and electricity, but with an area of just 300 square feet, plus a wraparound porch, the space holds only what they need or don't want to live without. For Peggy, that means the orchids she is growing on the windowsill; for both, their part-Lab dog named Bear.

Less Means Less Stress

Back to the Vacation House model. In a rented holiday space, your sense of relaxation is enhanced because there are fewer things to keep track of, and what you need is easily located. Rather than being overwhelmed by your environment, you feel in control. An interesting thing about a rented vacation house is that you aren't being judged by its size and contents, because they aren't *yours*. They are there to serve you, not vice versa. Your milieu, in its proper place, feels like an asset rather than a burden.

Your own home is a different situation in that it has the things you love in it, things that are imbued with a sentimental richness. But even then, there is a limit to how many you need to have surrounding you. It helps to think of your environment as subordinate to you, a backdrop to help your life flow smoothly and provide comfort and self-expression—not be an end in itself.

A simple example: In your vacation rental, there is a potato peeler in the shallow drawer beside the stove. You can always locate it because it has a definite home and because it is visible when you open the drawer. You return it to its spot when you are finished using it, because it is the only one, and you want to be able to find it again. At home, you have a potato peeler just like it. You also have the replacement potato peeler you bought last Thanksgiving when you could not find the first one, the cute peeler with the plastic handle painted like a ladybug that was a gift, and the "perfectly good" one you brought home when you were clearing out your great-aunt's home.

You see no reason to get rid of any of them. They're small, and they all work. Not that you have potatoes that often any more. . . . Still, when you multiply them by *all* the duplicates and extra things you have in your home that you don't find in a vacation space, there is a feeling of heaviness. Stuff is not neutral. It demands attention, weighs you down, causes stress when it mixes with all the other stuff, and you can't find it.

Less Frees Up Energy

The joy of pared-down spaces is that they physically require less of your time. If you have only a finite number of things, and they each have a place where they belong, you can find them easily and put them away. The problem of trying to find something you *know* you have but can't think where, besides being stressful, is that you end up disrupting other areas in your search, digging into cartons and drawers. Those places don't always get put back together right away. When you find what you were looking for, you go back to the project for which it was needed, leaving a history of your search behind.

Having less stuff to look after and a smaller area to keep clean leaves you with more energy for entertaining and doing things outside your home. It frees up emotional energy for you to go on vacation and not have to worry about someone burglarizing your things. You feel freer to go places and have new experiences since you aren't invested in caring for a lot of property.

Bob Reed, a longtime friend of Judi's in-laws, came to New York City after World War II. He worked in an insurance office in Manhattan and lived most of his adult life in the St. George Hotel in Brooklyn. But before you imagine him curling up and dying in one room, you should know that at 90, he was still working as an actuary, attending movie premieres, taking the train to visit family and friends, and loving life. He still walked miles through the city and knew the history of every historic building. If he hadn't broken his hip and developed pneumonia, there's no telling how much longer he might have continued that way. When Judi and Tom had dinner with him 2 months before he died, he ordered the most adventurous entrée on the menu, coconut shrimp; he was especially interested in hearing about their grandchildren, whom he had remembered generously at Christmas.

Less Means Less

Choosing to live in a smaller space means that you will not be *able* to continue as you were if you were a self-described pack rat. Adelaide Altman puts it succinctly in *Elderhouse* when she says, "You have no space now to house mediocrity, no odd corners or upstairs rooms to tuck away yesterday's big bargains and big mistakes." A time will come, if it has not already, when you will realize that truth with relief.

A schoolmate of ours, Vicki MacNeil Gould, described preparing to move into their newly built home: "So yesterday and today, I began the process of boxing up those items that weren't put into storage when we sold our prior house. I brought with me to this very small rental house items I was sure I could not live without, but in looking back over the 6 months we've lived here, many of these items haven't been touched. So once again, I'm weeding through my junk. I want a no-clutter look in this new house of ours . . . no cutesy knickknacks, no "fluff" or items that serve no purpose other than being fabulous dust collectors. I want clean lines in the new house . . . I want to keep it simple.

"This afternoon, as my toss pile began growing, I found myself wondering what my spirit life would look like if it were depicted as a furnished house. How much clutter would there be? Would my spirit house be filled with fluff but lack items that truly mattered? Would visitors to my spirit house be so overwhelmed with things that the purpose of the house lost its meaning? And would people feel free to visit my spirit house anytime, or would they feel compelled to schedule an appointment first because the resident of the house was so busy being busy, she lost track of people time?"

Less Is in the Details

Interestingly, you can spend the same amount of money building a condominium or small house as you can on one twice as large. The difference is in the amount of detail, personalization, and built-in cabinetry. Although a McMansion may give you two to three times the floor space, if the rooms are large, unfinished boxes, they will be hard to settle into emotionally. In her book, *The Not-So-Big House,* architect Sarah Susanka tells the story of a family who bought a piece of property they loved, with one condition imposed on them—that the contractor selling the land would be the one to build the house. They chose a design that looked, on paper, close to what they wanted; but when building started, and they saw the actual size, they wanted to scale it down.

The builder told them that making changes would cost a prohibitive amount of money, and since they were already at their limit, they decided to wait and see. They ended up spending $500,000 for an ostentatious, high-ceilinged box with 4,000 square feet and no soul. The unhappy couple sold the house and had one of 2,300 square feet created for them instead. Interestingly, it cost almost as much to complete as the original house. But it had customized built-in cabinetry including window seats and bookcases, a large amount of natural wood, and a cozy—rather than cold—family room where the adults could relax and the children play.

The moral is not that you need to spend a lot of money to have a place you feel comfortable in. If you start out knowing that a smaller area will make it easier to refine your space and give you what you truly want, you can skip the expensive mistakes. You will be able to customize the space yourself and make it a place where you want to spend time.

Less Helps the Earth

Remember ecology? There seems to be less of an emphasis on it these days, but that does not make the need to conserve resources any less urgent. At times, it seems as if we have learned nothing at all. But living in a smaller space, besides having emotional advantages, is good for the environment. Smaller houses using less land need fewer resources (read electricity and fossil fuel) to keep running. They are also giving off fewer pollutants. Although everyone has not yet gotten the message, more people are starting to look disdainfully at Hummers and other mega-vehicles and shudder when reading a magazine story about an 8,000-square-foot house built for two people.

As Daniel D. Chiras points out in *The Natural House,* "You won't find a robin with two nests, one for the chicks and the other to hold all the stuff."

TURNING FURNITURE INTO ADVENTURE

Perhaps you have inherited antiques from your family. Or, you were attracted to certain items and amassed collectibles that have become valuable. If so, you now have a choice. You can try to find a smaller place that will still accommodate everything, or you can decide that you want to shift into a different mode. The most practical—but perhaps least satisfying—path would be to scale down by selling some of your valuables, and put the money in the bank. Slightly above that would be to set aside everything for your children or younger relatives—whether they are interested in having them or not. But in our view, the most rewarding thing is to sell them for a fair price, then use the money for an exciting experience.

Even if you travel regularly, there may be adventures that you have not undertaken because of the cost. Now is the time to visit the Galapagos Islands or Antarctica, or take a trip around the world. If you haven't yet traveled, you can go anywhere. If you are not interested in roaming the world or are unable to do so physically, choose something closer to home. Perhaps you've always wanted a luxury car, but never owned one. Now is the time.

Of course, you can do something altruistic with the money realized. You can set up a college fund for younger family members. You can call Habitat for Humanity and see the results of your scaling down used to build a home for a family that would not otherwise have one. You can endow a scholarship for students at a community music school or art center.

Whatever you choose, consider it found money, apart from your regular income, and use it for something memorable. You'll look back in the future, glad that you did.

New Pleasures

Speaking of doing something exciting for yourself, when you move into a smaller space, it is satisfying to choose a place that has some luxury you did not have before. This may be a Jacuzzi bathtub, a balcony on a floor with a view of sunrises or sunsets, a gas fireplace, music speakers in every room, a greenhouse window (or window seat), convection oven, plasma TV, or wireless Internet access. It could also mean the convenience of having activities you love close at hand, such as a golf course, well-equipped gym and classes, or onsite restaurant. If you are involved in church activities, moving to within walking distance of your church will take away the inconvenience of having to drive there yourself or get a ride home.

Your new pleasure can also be an activity. In the last three historic estates and museums we visited, the docents each cheerfully mentioned that they were "beyond 80." You can be a docent at any age, of course, but these guides were finding it particularly zestful. They were excited about what they were describing and interested in relating to the group.

When Gordon and Mary moved to a condominium half the size of their rambling colonial home, the one thing he was reluctant to leave behind were his tools. Despite Mary's skepticism—"You're 75! You won't be making any repairs *here*"—Gordon stored them in their one-car garage. Without his large property to putter around, he started visiting shops and galleries with his wife. In one art gallery, when he saw an exquisite handcrafted table, something inside him stirred. He contacted the craftsman to express his admiration. Though he felt that making such furniture was beyond his abilities, he eventually arranged an informal apprenticeship and began to create small bowls and candlesticks.

Because Gordon's work was both beautiful and reasonably priced, people began bringing him special pieces of wood—often from a black walnut or cherry tree in their yard that had to be taken down. They would ask him to craft items for them. He did, letting the wood take the direction it wanted. After a year, he was invited to show at galleries on Cape Cod and Long Island.

Gordon has more projects planned than he can easily accomplish, and he loves his new life. He also feels that if they hadn't moved, he would still be busy puttering around, mowing his large lawn, repairing shingles, and all the other upkeep an older home demands. He would have missed the interest that is giving him one of the greatest satisfactions of his life.

YOUR NEW LIFE

So what is the next passion waiting for you? Consider what a shame it would be to miss the opportunity because you are mired in stuff and routine. The lighter you are living and the less encumbered you are, the easier it will be to move forward into a new adventure. In an inspiring book that is directed toward people age 40 and beyond, *It's Only Too Late If You Don't Start Now*, Barbara Sher gives advice and examples of how to "rediscover the inspired, enthusiastic adventurer you *wanted* to be before you became the responsible adult you *had* to be." She explains how maturity and being finished with the tasks of the first half of your life actually make it easier to explore your passions and dreams.

But you do need to meet your dreams halfway. All of us know people who lived in the same large home for 40 to 50 years, sticking to their old routines and refusing to leave until they were incapacitated and could no longer manage their daily lives. They were forced into a more restricted situation, leaving other people to pick up the pieces. Sadly, they were not emotionally prepared to start a new life and often died within the year.

Contrast that with Gordon's story where, by scaling down, he was able to focus on a new and thrilling life. It is a matter of letting go: of stuff, of the pride of "large," of preconceived ideas of what people at a certain age are able to do. When you do, you will find that "living large" is a fact of your life.

USING YOUR SPACE
FOR YOU

When many of us were setting up homes for the first time—beyond the brick-and-board bookcases, psychedelic posters, and parental hand-me-downs—we relied on established styles. We chose Early American or Victorian or French Provincial furniture, in part because it was sold in sets right down to the end tables and lamps, and in part, because these styles were familiar to us and "looked right." We bought maple spinning wheels that held plants, imitation crystal vases fit for Versailles, and a lot of brocade.

Later on, when we became more sophisticated, decorating magazines helped by showing kitchens filled with old crocks and advertising tins, china cabinets crammed with Blue Willow dishes and Staffordshire dogs, whitewashed walls with the folk art of Santa Fe. The rooms looked charming and gave us a new direction; we traded in our cheap imitations for the real thing and wondered how we could ever have been so undiscerning.

Around this time, many of us were buying our first homes—homes whose rooms already had designated purposes, such as the living room, the breakfast nook, the "Florida room." Along with the designation came the assumption that you would decorate them according to their titles. Even though you may have had a black thumb and little interest in watering anything, you bought plants for the "sunroom" because plants were what belonged in a sunroom. You put linens in the linen closet, even though it might not have been the most convenient place to store tablecloths or sheets.

We accepted the conventional use of space and how a room should be decorated without asking questions. Some of us gave up completely and relied on the expertise of decorators or family members.

It was probably necessary to go through those stages to get to the place you are now, to where you know what you want and need. Whether you are moving to a new home and starting with a blank canvas or reconfiguring your current home or apartment, you can make the space do exactly what you want. Although you need a restful place to sleep and a bathroom for the usual purposes, everything else is up for grabs. If, as was recently proclaimed by Lauren Hutton on the cover of AARP magazine, "Sixty is the new thirty," you are being given a second chance at creating your environment.

MOVING INTO A NEW SPACE

The least rewarding thing you can do if you are moving is to try to fit the same furniture into the same configurations as in your present home. Note that we said "least rewarding." There is nothing *wrong* with trying to replicate your current environment and use of space except that it may not work well in a smaller area. More important, you will be missing out on a great adventure. You no longer have to ask, "What will fit?" but "Will it work with what I *really* want?"

First Steps

Rather than analyzing or writing anything down at first, find a comfortable chair, and sit and mull it over. Mulling is the equivalent of doodling on a piece of paper, letting your mind go where it will, letting it make whatever connections it wants to make. Don't censor any ideas. Later, you will need to answer the following questions, but you can use them now as jumping-off points. If you live with other people, include them in your imagining as well:

What do I need emotionally from the place I live?

What are the activities I love doing most?

What would make me happy to never have to do again?

What seems like underutilized or wasted space?

If my living room or bedroom could be anything at all, I would like . . .

Are these easy things to think about? Of course not. Analysis takes energy and involves making choices. This is why we suggest approaching your preferences from your more intuitive right brain and not in 1-2-3 order.

Meet—And Beat—The Resistors

As soon as you realize that this process is leading to making choices and having to act on them, out come the Resistors. These are not simply negatives meant to spoil your fun. They are dedicated to protecting you—to stopping you from making mistakes *and* keeping you in your comfort zone. But sometimes they are overzealous in ridiculing new ideas in order to keep you on a safe path. Before you move on, take a look at some of the main Resistors:

" I don't want to make any changes that would hurt my home's resale value."

This statement strikes us as sad. It is similar to someone buying a new car, then saying, "I'm only going to drive it when my other car is in the shop, because I want to keep the mileage low for the trade-in." That attitude makes you the caretaker of the property, keeping it nice for some future owner, instead of behaving like it's *yours*. If you've always dreamed of a vaulted-ceiling library, and your garage is the perfect place to create one, why not do so? You'll have years of pleasure, and if you or your heirs get a little less because it's too nice to park a car in, your satisfaction is worth the difference. Most of the time individualizing a space actually adds to the selling price. But even if it doesn't, don't sell *yourself* short.

" I wouldn't have the nerve."

We are not talking about climbing the Himalayas here or rushing into a burning building to save children. Painting a mural on the kitchen wall or turning your dining room into a Parisian cafe, making your balcony a Zen retreat or your living room into a playhouse for your grandchildren does not require nerves of steel. Although making changes can feel risky and take you out of your comfort zone, don't accept that you "don't have the nerve." Almost anything can be repainted or restored to the way it was if you don't like the way it has turned out, or you change your mind.

" My landlord/the facility won't let me do anything wild."

Some places are restrictive about allowing you to make structural changes or even changing the white paint on the walls. But there are many ways to create an ambiance by the way you use furniture, lighting, designation of room purpose, and so on. If you have always wanted a soothing bedroom retreat, you can create it by having a very comfortable bed and covering it with soft linens, then installing a tabletop fountain with a calming water sound, subtle lighting or candles, and a plug-in scent you enjoy. Creating a space that engages your senses does not have to involve drastic changes.

" I don't have the money to do it."

If you have the time, there are many ingenious changes that you can make yourself with a very small cash outlay. With bonding tape and hot glue guns available, you don't even need to know how to sew. Furniture can be given a whole new feeling by painting it, and your local library shelves are filled with books on thrifty decorating. One that we like is *Design on a Dime,* but you will find a wide assortment.

Sometimes, "I don't have the money to do it," actually means, "I don't want to be bothered."

" I wouldn't know where to start."

Again, decorating books are almost as plentiful as cookbooks and are geared to all different tastes and incomes. Cable television has programs on such channels as HGTV (Home and Garden TV), DIY (Do It Yourself Network), Lifestyle, and many others that give step-by-step demonstrations. Spend an afternoon browsing in a good-size bookstore to get an idea of what appeals to you most, and buy a book that shows you how to do it. But the real place to start is with yourself, by addressing the concerns above and below.

" The space is too small."

This is the area where making choices comes into play. Even in a worst-case scenario such as having only a 10 by 10-foot space, you can still make it satisfying to yourself. Later in the chapter, we will discuss furniture with more than one use, such as a screen that not only hides something you find unattractive but can create a mood by displaying personal photographs or art postcards. In the old mission in Carmel, California, you can look into the tiny rooms where the Franciscan brothers lived. The whitewashed walls and simple furnishings, with perhaps only a colorful blanket or a santo for decoration, have a beauty and a mood all their own.

Your space is probably not as small as that, but the mission demonstrates that no rooms are too tiny to have them the way you want.

" People will think I'm crazy."

If this is something that seriously bothers you, be reassured that it is rarely true. If anything, people will be envious that you have the personal security and freedom to live exactly as you want. If some of your happiest memories are eating in a diner with red vinyl booths and table jukeboxes, why not be able to eat in one every day? If you want to keep your quilting frame and materials in the middle of the living room so you can let your friends see what you are working on and get involved if they want, go ahead and do it. Far from thinking you are crazy, people will be impressed that you are following your passion.

" There are too many necessities to be able to make it fun."

Perhaps you need to redefine necessities. If you have ever gone camping, you know that the only "necessities" are a sleeping bag, a place to keep your clothes and personal belongings such as a duffel bag, and a few dishes and utensils. A gas stove is helpful, but if there is already a fire pit, you don't even need that.

Judi's aunt, the wife of a Presbyterian minister in Michigan, did not enjoy entertaining. During their ministry, she avoided having people over for dinner unless she had no choice. When her husband retired, they moved to Henry Ford Village, and her whole attitude changed. Once she found she could invite people for dinner and be served a delightful meal in the facility's dining room, she began to do so often. The kitchen in their unit held only the basics for simple meals for themselves, and she used the cabinets for storing other things—freeing up much more space for their beloved books and travel mementos.

" I'm not interested in fancy decorating."

The term "fancy decorating" implies ball-fringe lampshades, window "treatments," and furniture that looks like it belongs in Hearst Castle. But consider the case of Mac, who moved to a condo with his wife, Ellen. In their previous home, he kept his HO gauge model railroads in the basement; the rest of their house was conventionally decorated. In their new condo, however, he claimed one half of the built-in bookshelves in the living room to display his most interesting train models and paraphernalia. On the adjoining wall, he planned to hang several railroad-related prints and other memorabilia.

Ellen's initial reaction was dismay. She had planned to recreate a tasteful living room with *books* on the bookshelves, interspersed with appropriate art objects, and a formal seating area. She had assumed that their friends would come in, look around, and say, "Isn't this lovely?"—as usual. But she had to recognize the justice of Mac's claim; they no longer had a basement for him to express his passion. In fact, she began to think about what she might want to place on the other side of the bookshelves and, because she was interested in genealogy, decided to display old photographs, and family heirlooms. She framed her father's family christening gown in a shadow box on the adjoining wall. Now their friends come in and say, "This is fascinating!"

The point is that what we are suggesting is not about "fancy decorating." It is about pleasing yourself.

" I like things the way they are."

This objection implies that you have either been working on your living space for years and have perfected it—or that you just don't want to be bothered. At the risk of sounding sexist, we would expect the second reason to be more of a male one, although there are some women who have little interest in their environment. But why not go through the questions about your new space repeated in the next section, and see if there is any small change you would like to make to make your life more satisfying?

"Thinking about concepts like these is too hard. I don't want to do it."
It can be daunting if you try to think about big changes all at once.

But it can be fun to think about what you *would* want in your new or stream-lined home. If you are married or living with other people, they will have ideas as well. If, like Judi's Aunt Margaret, you no longer enjoy at-home entertaining and are moving to a complex that offers meals for you and guests, plan to grow the orchids you've always wanted to in the dining area, and leave the KitchenAid behind.

One of the questions we suggest for you to consider has to do with what you *never* want to do again. If your nemesis is "hauling garbage cans to the curb" or "fertilizing the lawn," look for a space where you are not responsible for either task. If it is an indoor job such as "changing the kitty litter" or "vacuuming rugs," consider splurging on one of the cat boxes that disposes of the waste automatically or one of those robots that hums around your floors vacuuming everything. We live in an age when an amazing number of conveniences exist, some of which you may not even be aware of.

Mull, Then Write

After you have mulled over some of these questions and fantasized exactly what you would like to have in your space, take a pen and paper, and answer the following questions:

What do I need emotionally from the place where I live?

What are the activities I love doing most?

What would make me happy to never have to do again?

What seems like underutilized or wasted space?

If my living room or bedroom could be anything at all, I would like . . . .

Whether you are planning to move or to reconfigure your present space, your answers can help you focus in on the changes you want to make. The last four United States censuses have found that only 4.5 percent of retirees now move across state lines, making an overwhelming 95-plus percent who are not heading for Florida or North Carolina or Arizona. They are staying close to where they worked, raised a family, and developed friendships and community ties. They are doing this in several ways. In 2002, for the first time, the sale of condominiums outstripped the sale of single-family homes. Condos situated on one floor, with quality fixtures and all the amenities—but not necessarily in a "senior community"—were especially desirable. Their purchasers are going for large kitchens and entertainment spaces, and they appreciate rooms with built-in Internet connections and adequate outlets that can be used for offices. Many people have no desire to retire completely.

A condominium or an apartment on one floor in an elevator building is a good choice because it anticipates future needs by eliminating stairs. It also eliminates lawn care and outdoor maintenance at a time when many people are happy to exchange that for gardening on a balcony or sunny window. When there are problems, there are other people you can call about fixing them. If traveling is your main interest, you can have a space that does not require a lot of maintenance, but has adequate room to show off your world treasures. In the last chapter, we gave suggestions for other amenities you may not have had or thought about having before.

Spacing Out

If you live with someone else, it is crucial for each of you to have your own space to which to retreat. No matter how convivial you are, you each need a place where you can sit, undisturbed, to read or think or pursue your creative passions. When the poet, Diana Chang, moved to a complex with her husband, they decided to each get their own unit, next door to each other, rather than share the same apartment. If you feel that space is at a premium, even part of a room—or an alcove—protected by a screen or large plants can work. The point is that this is a place where you will be undisturbed.

While we are on the subject of space, if you are moving into a compact area, there is even less reason to have one-purpose rooms. This is an area where you can be as creative as you want. Consider the following, which we have seen successfully combined: greenhouse/kitchen; dining room/library; living room/art gallery; balcony/Moroccan dining tent; dining room/piano bar; guest room/art studio; bedroom/movie theater; bathroom/darkroom. Remember that it is up to you to decide what you want in your space.

Furniture should also be encouraged to have more than one use. If you have pared down, you can get rid of bulky storage items such as dining room buffets and dainty "desks" that do not hold a lot, but take up valuable space. The same is true of bedside and end tables that have no storage space, and table lamps that need a place on which to perch. Attractive wooden file cabinets can double as nightstands or desk pillars. If it doesn't pull its weight, a piece of furniture needs to be extremely beautiful or unique to have a spot in your new home.

Another consideration is the way you decorate. Realtor and residential building contractor, Jane Best, explains it this way:

"Imagine a new, empty home with a living room that has off-white walls, ceiling, carpet. It looks large because the eye can flow easily throughout the room. Then place a 9 by 9-foot deep purple throw rug in the center of the room. Immediately, it becomes the focal point and makes the room look smaller. Then place some dark mahogany furniture against the off-white walls. That breaks up the space on the wall and makes the room appear even smaller. Then add some plaid wallpaper. Still smaller. The more stuff in the room and the more contrasting colors, the smaller the room will appear."

She adds, "One of the tips real estate agents give to homeowners when they are getting ready to show and sell their homes is to take as much furniture, accessories, and clutter out of their rooms as possible because the more stuff that is in a room, the smaller the room appears."

STAYING PUT

In the opening months of 2004, empty nesters and single parents between the ages of 50 and 64 with no children under 18 at home accounted for nearly a quarter of all spending on home improvements. Much of the money spent was to convert basements, children's bedrooms, junk rooms, or "wasted space" into something else—offices, craft or music studios, walk-in closets, meditation or exercise rooms, greenhouses, or simply retreats. These people were staying put and improving their existing homes and apartments. They were ready to have it their way—sometimes by expanding but often by simply reconfiguring the space.

Take a House Tour

If you are uncertain how to begin, go through your home and make notes. In each room, think about the following:

- What is this room used for?

- What is its ambiance, the feeling that it gives people?

- What percentage of the time is it in use?

- What is the best thing you can imagine the room could be?

- What would have to be done to create it that way?

Suppose one room you chose to answer these questions about was your large basement. The answer to the first question might be, "Doing the laundry and storing junk" and to the second, a fit of hysterical laughter imagining what style a hanging light bulb and ceiling with drooping pink insulation could have. The answer to the third question is probably "Not much." But then there's the last two questions, which invite your imagination to take over. Maybe you see it as divided into areas: a workbench and tools to work on furniture; another area for art projects or dancing; the laundry, of course, and then a small, separate section for items you have to save. To get it that way, you would have to have a ceiling and lighting put in, some vinyl tile flooring, which you could install yourself, and then the finishing touches you want. For well under $10,000, you have 500 more usable square feet.

If you analyzed the guest room, which already has a pleasant ambiance, you may have found that it is actually used less than 4 percent of the time (based on company staying in it for 2 weeks a year). If you need an office, a meditation room, an exercise space, art studio, or any number of other places, here is where you should look. You may decide on anything from a pull-down bed to a convertible couch that you could use the rest of the time. People often feel that they need to expand and add on these special rooms as offices or studios, when what they actually need is to examine their current home usage more carefully.

A personal example: For years, Judi had wanted a sunroom overlooking the backyard and woods beyond. She and Tom wanted it to be a natural part of the house but could not decide on where it should be attached. Spending $40,000 for a small add-on gazebo seemed wasteful, anyway. Finally Judi thought of the pantry between the kitchen and the garage, a 9 by 9-foot area of little charm. Since it was her project, she demolished the pantry door, ceiling-high shelves and studs (after making sure they were not weight bearing), took the doors off several ugly kitchen-style wood cabinets across from the pantry and painted the shelves yellow.

A custom window the length of the outer wall was installed where the pantry had been, next to a single French door. An attractive light fixture was added to the ceiling by an electrician. Judi tiled the floor and painted the walls, including a faux brick treatment on one. She also found some decorative Italian tiles and created a dining table, topping it with glass and painting thrift shop wrought-iron chairs to match. Cookbooks and decorative items went on the open shelves, as well as lots of plants. The sunroom has given her great satisfaction and a lot of use; when people see the space, which cost around $3,000 to restore and completely furnish, the word they most often use is "magical."

To get the room of her dreams, Judi had to give up five enclosed pantry shelves and three eye-level storage cabinets. It meant adding shelves to a broom closet in the kitchen for foodstuffs, storing garden items in the basement, and scaling down china, glassware, and kitchen utensils even further. But trading dead "stuff" for a vibrant living area seemed a no-brainer.

Thinking about what is truly important to you and summoning up a little courage can lead to the spaces of your dreams as well.

Another Mission Statement

This is a good place for a new mission statement, one that is focused on the opportunity you have to start anew. We call this the Living Large Mission Statement. The Living Large Mission Statement helps you identify the possibilities for growth and adventure, acknowledge your obstacles and doubts, and commit to making your dreams come true. Here are some examples.

I want to . . .

● Travel and study art

● Have money to do interesting things

● Sail my boat through the Caribbean

● Start a children's theater group

● Trade-in mowing the lawn

● Join the Peace Corps

● Live in a little beach cottage

But . . .

● I don't know how to get started

● I think I'm too old

● I have a large mortgage

● I have too much stuff to fit

● I don't have the nerve

So I will . . .

● Downscale everything and put what I can't part with in temporary storage

● Find a smaller, less-expensive home in an area I love

● Talk to people who have done what I want to do, and find out how they managed

● Realize in this new world, age is no longer an issue

● Take small steps to get my nerve back

Now it's your turn to start up this next stage in your life.

*I want to*_____

_____

_____

But _____

_____

_____

*So I will*_____

_____

_____

This is a different journey, perhaps a more pleasureable one, and a reward for your hard work. We would love to hear about your progress, both in scaling down and living large. You can e-mail Judi at ScalingDown@att.net and Marj at TimeIsPriceless@juno.com or write to us in care of Rodale (33 E. Minor Street, Emmaus, Pennsylvania 18098).

Meanwhile, we are confident you are heading into the most rewarding time of your life!

additional sources

Just as libraries have expanded their offerings, we recognize that there are many ways to get help. Here are a few valuable resources:

• ClutterFreeLiving.com is a Web site filled with articles and solid advice.

• The Container Store has stores all over America but also offers extensive products at thecontainerstore.com. Or call 888-CONTAIN for a store near you.

• Hold Everything is one of the original venues for organizing supplies. Phone 800-421-2285 for a catalog or the location of a store near you.

• Home Focus on Neat and Clean Living. Call 800-221-6771 for a catalog of helpful products.

• Jeff Campbell's Clean Team explains how to have time left over for living by using intelligent methods and products. Call 800-717-2532 for a catalog or visit cleanteam.com.

• Lillian Vernon offers many organizing supplies as well as other interesting items. Visit lillianvernon.com or call 800-901-9291 for a catalog.

• National Organization of Professional Organizers can be contacted at 512-206-0151. If you visit their Web site at napo.com, you can type in your zip code and see a list of professional organizers near you and what specific services they offer.

• OrganizeEverything.com is a Web site that sells everything for organizing that you can imagine and a few things you never thought about.

• Stacks and Stacks Homewares has storage with a flair. Its retail store is located in San Francisco, but you can call 800-761-5222 for a catalog.

bibliography

Altman, Adelaide. *Elderhouse.* Vermont: Chelsea Green, 2002.

Aslett, Don. *Clutter's Last Stand.* Cincinnati: Writer's Digest, 1984.

Aslett, Don. *Not for Packrats Only.* New York: Penguin Books, 1991.

Baird, Lori, ed. *Cut the Clutter and Stow the Stuff.* Emmaus, PA: Rodale, 2002.

Beckerman, Ilene. *Love, Loss, and What I Wore.* Chapel Hill: Algonquin Books, 1995.

Chiras, Daniel D. *The Natural House.* Vermont: Chelsea Green, 2000.

Cilley, Marla. *Kitchen Sink Reflections.* New York: Bantam Books, 2002.

Collins, Terah Kathryn. *The Western Guide to Feng Shui.* Carlsbad, CA: Hay House, 1996.

DeGraaf, John, David Wann, and Thomas H. Naylor. *Affluenza, The All-Consuming Epidemic.* San Francisco: Berrett-Koehler Publishers, 2001.

Dominguez, Joe, and Vicki Robin. *Your Money or Your Life.* New York: Penguin Putnam, 1992.

Ellis, Estelle, Caroline Seebohm, and Christopher Simon Sykes. *At Home with Books, How Booklovers Live with and Care for Their Libraries.* New York: Carol Southern Books, 1995.

Ferrer, Christy. *Breaking the Rules, Home Style for the Way We Live Today.* New York: Simon & Schuster, 2001.

Hetzer, Linda, and Janet Hulstrand. *Moving On, A Practical Guide to Downsizing the Family Home.* New York: Stewart, Tabori, and Chang, 2004.

HGTV Books. *Design on a Dime.* Des Moines: Meredith Books, 2003.

Katillac, Kelee. *House of Belief, Creating Your Personal Style.* Salt Lake City: Gibbs-Smith, 2000.

Kingston, Karen. *Clear Your Clutter with Feng Shui.* New York: Broadway Books, 1999.

Kinsel, Brenda. *Brenda's Wardrobe Companion: A Guide to Getting Dressed from the Inside Out.* Berkeley, CA: Wildcat Canyon Press, 2003.

Lawson, Todd, and Tom Connor. *The House to Ourselves, Reinventing Home Once the Kids Are Grown.* Newtown, CT: Taunton Press, 2004.

Madden, Chris Casson. *A Room of Her Own, Women's Personal Spaces.* New York: Clarkson Potter, 1997.

Michels, Richard, ed. *Collector's Styles, Decorating with the Things You Love.* Des Moines: Meredith Books, 2002.

Schor, Juliet B. *The Overspent American, Why We Want What We Don't Need.* New York: Basic Books, 1998.

Sher, Barbara. *It's Only Too Late If You Don't Start Now.* New York: Delacorte, 1998.

St. James, Elaine. *Simplify Your Life.* New York: Hyperion, 1994.

Stanley, Thomas J., and William D. Danko. *The Millionaire Next Door.* New York: Simon & Schuster, 1996.

Starr, Meryl. *The Home Organizing Workbook.* San Francisco: Chronicle Books, 2004.

Susanka, Sarah. *The Not So Big House.* Newtown, CT: Taunton Press, 1998.

Zakas, Spiros. *Lifespace, A New Approach to Home Design.* New York: Macmillan, 1977.

index

d

e

f